The Life and the Way

THE CHRISTIAN YOGA METAPHYSICS

BY

A. K. MOZUMDAR

Founder of the Christian Yoga Society

THE BOOK TREE

SAN DIEGO, CALIFORNIA

Originally published 1911
Christian Yoga Society
New York

Reprinted from the First Edition
New material, revisions and cover
©2002
The Book Tree
All rights reserved

ISBN 1-58509-040-9

Cover layout and design
Lee Berube

Printed on Acid-Free Paper
in the United States and United Kingdom
by LightningSource, Inc.

Published by
The Book Tree
P O Box 16476
San Diego, CA 92176

We provide fascinating and educational products to help awaken the public to new ideas and
information that would not be available otherwise.
Call 1 (800) 700-8733 for our *FREE BOOK TREE CATALOG*.

INTRODUCTION

A. K. Mozumdar has written a number of spiritual classics that are sometimes not easy to find. Mozumdar was the founder of the Christian Yoga Society and created a system of thought, or philosophy, for it that is presented in this book.

At first glance it seems that Christian Yoga is a contradiction of terms. Most would believe that systems from the East and West, such as these, are not compatible enough to be enjoined into one metaphysical philosophy but Mozumdar does a masterful job in bridging the gap and bringing them both together. He was a man in touch with the all-embracing God-consciousness—enough to recognize and experience an all-pervading Oneness in the universe. This Oneness transcends religious separation and cultural barriers, which is what brought about the creation of the Christian Yoga Society.

The first half of this book details the general philosophy of the Society, and is entitled "The Way to Life or to Health, Happiness and Divine Oneness." Mozumdar uses not only his own teachings, but includes those of Jesus and the Buddha as well. Following this, a deep understanding of Christian Yoga can be realized through the question and answer process presented in the chapter called "The Light of Christian Yoga." One of the important concepts explained here and elsewhere in the book is that our perception of good and evil must be completely reconsidered. One has more power over evil and its influence than previously thought or accepted. This "power" over outside forces can be applied to other areas as well, giving one far more control over life and happiness than previously imagined.

The last three chapters of the book contain sayings or short paragraphs that provide clear philosophical knowledge and powerful guidelines of wisdom for daily living. On the surface, the book seems to be of a mystical or religious type, yet a deeper study of its contents would put it into the category or psychology and self-help—provided one uses it in the way it is intended.

This is an important book, as it is capable of helping to transform an individual. It is capable of providing the reader with a unique path to follow, and to achieve spiritual peace of mind.

Paul Tice

"As man thinketh in his heart so is he."

"As a piece of iron put in the furnace takes the quality of the fire, so our mind conceiving the divine Ideal partakes of its attributes."   *Christian Yoga Metaphysics.*

"Without the glass there is no possibility of a sight of the reflection: whence then could there be any possibility of the knowledge of name and form without assuming that which is Existence, Consciousness, and Bliss?"

Panchadasi, Upanishad.

"The Seer of thy sight thou shalt not see; the Hearer of thy ear thou shalt not hear; the Thinker of thy thoughts thou shalt not think; the Knower of thy knowledge thou shalt not know— this is thy Real Self, all-pervading, everything besides is but mortal."   *Brhadaranyakopanishad.*

"Verily I say unto you, Except ye be converted, and become as little children, ye shall not enter into the kingdom of heaven. Whosoever therefore shall humble himself as this little child, the same is greatest in the kingdom of heaven."

Matthew 18 : 3-4.

"Marvel not that I say unto thee, Ye must be born again. Verily, verily, I say unto thee, Except a man be born again, he cannot see the kingdom of God."   *John* 3 :7-3.

CONTENTS

PREFACE

The author sends this treatise into the world in the name of the Great Ideal, through whose inspiration he undertook to write it. Excepting the first few pages this book was written inside of a month, in the midst of repeated interruptions by visitors, students and friends. Without the Divine inspiration and guidance it would have been impossible for the author to write this metaphysics, in the midst of a strenuous, busy life, and in a language which he had acquired in but a short time, by self study. By the above statement he does not mean to underrate the value of an academic education, he simply wants to convey the idea that the Almighty can do His work even through one who has very little or no education in the academic sense. That fact alone ought to be a message of hope to many millions of God loving souls, who are willing to work in the Lord's vineyard, yet who are hampered by the feeling of their inability and limitation. After writing this treatise, the author has been more than convinced, that to understand the divine philosophy of life, there is very little need of academic education. The education which we receive in the Almighty's kindergarten by the simple trust and self-surrender is sufficient for that purpose. The secret of work in the field of truth is the simple trust in the All-providing power within us. The scientific explanation of the word trust has been given in this metaphysics. If any one is willing to know about the great mystery of life, let him or her read this book over and over again.

It is shown in this treatise that the power and efficiency of our personal will is very limited, compared with the great Cosmic Will, which by our divine rights we are able to manifest. The man who is constantly conscious of his limitation cannot possibly manifest unlimited power. He cannot rely upon his limited will to manifest unlimited power. Granting that by the proper training we can develop our personal will, we cannot assume that we can develop it without limit. Suppose that we continue to affirm that our will power is unlimited, even then, we cannot hope to get the best results if we do not fully comprehend the meaning of our affirmation. It is not so much the question of affirmation, but of realization that we have an unlimited will power that gives us the power. Very few can have that concept of limitless power of their personal will starting from their limited concept of life. It has been observed that many people starting with the assumption of the unlimited power of the human will had to come back to testify against that philosophy. The fault lies not with the philosophy, but in their understanding. There exists only one power in this universe. Our personal power belongs to that power, and is only detached in our consciousness. To establish unity with that Cosmic power by our conscious realization is the main purpose of this life. We have to establish unity, but we have not yet accomplished that purpose. We are certainly limited now, though unlimited power lies before us. With this concept of limitation the only way we can manifest limitless power is by trusting in and self-surrendering ourselves to the unlimited Divine Will. The author had the inspiration to the effect, that we manifest power by the quality of thought, and not by any assumption of meaningless affirmation. When we are thoroughly absorbed with the thought that the power of our Great Ideal is manifesting through us, we do not care whether we have any power or not. That is the time we really manifest power. The less conscious we are of ourselves by the higher quality of thought, the more we become or manifest that quality. Demonstration was made in the case of a man who could not walk without crutches for two years. When he grasped the idea that his limbs belonged to the Great God and they were under His control his mind was relieved of the consciousness that he could not walk. No sooner had his mind become free, than he walked. Several similar demonstrations were carried out successfully. Hence this metaphysics is no longer an experimental science. It is a new revelation. Those who are ready will receive new light from this treatise. The author does not claim any credit for this work, all credit is due to the Almighty power which has directed him to follow its mandates. Therefore judge not this work by the light of the author's life, but judge it in the light of the Truth. Let peace be with all.

A. K. Mozumdar.

The Way To Life

or

To Health, Happiness and Divine Oneness

There is no evil, because God is All good and All in All. There cannot be anything beyond God. No two contradictory forces such as good and evil can exist in the same universe, if one is omnipresent and all powerful. Consequently there is no such condition or force called evil, as opposed to good, because God is good and omnipresent. Why then let your mind be forced into the error-thought by admitting error, and into the fear-thought by admitting evil. If "there is nothing either good or bad, but thinking makes it so" why then think such things as evil, mortality, disease and death. If it is all concept, all thought, then, let us have the concept of immortality, All good, All health, All life. If anyone commits evil, it is because he thinks evil and believes evil. The true interpretation of an action is the motive which actuates it. Hence, we say, no one can perpetrate an evil deed without knowing that evil. We know evil by accepting it in the popular sense and thinking of it. The fall of man from Paradise is caused by his acceptance or knowledge of evil. The first man, whoever he might have been, was banished from his God-consciousness by his own wrong thinking. Had he known, it is the thought or the consciousness that makes a man what he is, he never would have surrendered his divine heritage, the God-consciousness. As we know evil by thinking, so we know good also by thinking. If we believe that good overcometh

13

evil, then we ought to think good or the thought of good. Because as we think so we become. It is an error-thought, that without knowing evil we cannot know good. Because in the first place we have admitted that there is no evil, our thinking makes the evil. Hence, it will not be necessary to think evil in order to think good. Now in a comparative sense, if we call yesterday's good evil, on account of our better understanding to-day, then that evil is not something opposed to good. If evil means less good in the relative sense, it cannot have an opposite effect to that of good. If the evil which we expect comes to us with its evil effect, it is because we believe in it. No effect is good or bad but our thinking makes it so. If we know how to put a different meaning to an effect which we call evil, we can turn it into a good effect. So long as we do not manifest the perfect good, we are bound to have all kinds of experiences. These experiences can not be anything but good. In the relative plane we generally consider our better understanding good. Even then, why should we consider our past experiences, which were necessary for our present better understanding, evil. In this relative plane everything is good in its place. Even to exist in this plane we must exist in God and manifest God-life. If we manifest less God-life than we ought to, according to our understanding, we cannot say, that we do not manifest any God-life whatever. There being only one Life, if it is a Life at all, it must be the God-life. Everything in that Life is grand and beautiful; there cannot be any evil. Evil there is none in this world of perfection and all-good. If anyone finds evil his thinking makes it so. Then if any of you would say, that by the denial of evil we have admitted it, since we cannot deny a thing without admitting its existence, the answer would be then, admit evil as imperfect good, and not negation of good. There cannot be anything or any place where there is no good.

Evil simply means the imperfect manifestation of good. Since by the word evil we understand absence of good, we would rather use the word imperfect good in its place. Some people want to be good by fighting evil. They know from their experiences that it is not an easy task. They ought to remember this, that they cannot fight the evil which their own thought creates. The thought which creates evil cannot fight against itself by creating an opposition. It is almost impossible to conquer evil that way. Though some people may succeed for the time being in keeping it down, in their unguarded moments it is bound to reappear. It is not quite as bad as to live in the constant dread of evil. "Resist no evil" has a deeper significance than the average people comprehend. The less a person resists evil the less he thinks about it. By thinking less he reduces its influence over him, because we partake of the nature of a thought we think. By the thought of good, grand and beautiful, we imbibe those qualities.

If we call a thing or a condition good it is always good, and it cannot be evil or bad. If bad means the less good, even then we cannot deny that it is good after all. The man who cannot see good in the evil is the moral victim of evil. That does not mean that we have to live or approve the life below our better understanding; it simply means we should not hold any antagonistic thought towards the evil. If we hold the antagonistic thought toward evil we are liable to invite the evil to our thought realm which may force us to do more evil in our reform act. Allowance we must make for the deeds of our brothers and sisters, not with the spirit of encouraging the evil, but with the spirit of inspiring good in them. By holding the thought against others, we not only give them the bad suggestion but also we take the very condition we are opposed to. If the moral teachers are good it is not because they condemn the evil, but because they live and think the moral life. Those who constantly condemn evil are often seen to commit evil in some form or other. Many a time their very act of reform leads them to adopt such means which call for reform in themselves.

One who lives in the constant dread of evil lacks moral courage to shake off the shackles of evil. It haunts him like his own shadow. The less conscious we are of evil the less evil we commit. By trying to see good in everything we inspire a better condition within us. It is the condition of calmness and peace, and the abiding rest and the feeling of security that guide us in the pathway of Heaven.

Who stops to think that man imperils his life-boat in the restless tempest of his feeling? Danger there is none. The only danger abides in his thought. Let him wake up his sleeping Master-nature; it will pacify the stormy sea of life. He will hear again the Master Jesus speak through his soul, "Oh, ye of little faith!" Ah, my friends, this life is simply grand and beautiful when you understand it. Have you forgotten what the Master said, "Unto you it is given to know the mystery of the kingdom of God; but unto them that are without, all these things are done in parables."

Everywhere we hear the stories of disease and suffering, most of which are caused by the restlessness and fear-thought. In order to have peace we must know, that it is our divine prerogative to demand or ask of the law of supply whatever we need. The rest leave in the hand of the Great God, who is within us and who is the soul of our soul. He always supplies our demand if we know how to demand. When we demand we must demand like a simple child. Care not whether your demand is fulfilled or not. The simple trust, that whatever that Law does is all right, will secure peace and calmness for you. Not that the Law is arbitrary, but that it needs a certain condition to work through. Whenever our mind is calm and undisturbed we come in touch with that Cosmic power whose part we are. When you suffer from any ailment command it to leave. Then hold the idea that you are going to live your own life; let the Great universal power All-health take care of the rest. The best of all thoughts is to give all your cares and troubles to the Almighty and trust in His protecting power. If you can lay down your pains and aches before God, and live a free, unconcerned life, you will make demonstrations which will surpass all your expectations. Hear the voice of God within you, the kingdom of Heaven is at hand.

II

We must first try to understand our relation with the Divine Life before we can use our Divine prerogative to demand. Before we demand anything of the Great Universal Law of supply we must know what right we have to do so. When we know our life and its desires all belong to God we are justified in demanding what belongs to us by Divine rights. That which is in God belongs to us, because we belong to Him. God does not own us in the sense of ownership, but He owns us as His own life. So what there is in God-life is also in our life in part. The more God-life we manifest the more we come to share all that there is in that life. They say our every positive demand is fulfilled. The positive demand does not mean the demand with a certain amount of force; it means the demand with the proper understanding of the law of life. To the extent we understand the law and our Divine rights do we become positive. The doubting mind is negative, because it lacks understanding. We never doubt regarding a thing which we positively know is coming to us. All knowledge is positive. It always insures within us calmness and peace. We know both by reason and intuition that in this universe there exists only one All-pervading Life. And our life is part expression of that Life. And our power and efficiency are determined by the degree of God-life we manifest. With the understanding of this Great Law of Life we come to abide in trust and peace. Gradually we wake up to the fact that the whole universe is within us, and every atom of it is vibrating with our life. In order to understand our Greater Life we must surrender our smaller life. Our concept is our life. We cannot have the greater concept without giving up our smaller concept. No concept is greater than the concept that our life belongs to the Great Universal Life. By giving ourselves to the Great concept of life we draw to ourselves, or become that concept. So the Master Jesus struck the highest note of Life when He urged the people to give everything to the Lord, even their very lives. He himself took no credit for what He did. He gave everything to God. Thereby He kept His highest concept of Life awake. He knew full well, as man thinketh in his heart so is he. Not that he believed God to be a distinct personality, but that He believed Him to be His greater life. By the universal concept of God and by the thought of Him He was able to live in the God-consciousness. We merge into our Ideal by constantly thinking it, as a living and moving power. When our Ideal is not only an Ideal in thought, but also an Ideal, which acts and moves through us like a living personality, we embody that Ideal. Then we cease to exist as it were and our Ideal becomes the real personality. The Master by giving everything to God, His grandest concept of Life, became God in His concept. He ceased to exist as a man of flesh, that is, as a man of limited concept, and lived the God-life according to His highest concept. The secret of our lives can be summed up in one idea, and it is this: that we become our Ideal by letting it manifest through us.

It is very hard to be what we think we are not, even by affirmation. Because on account of our consciousness of want, we fail to realize what we want to be. It sometimes disturbs our mental condition and increases our anxiety. Sometimes fear is liable to creep into our mind as to whether or not we will ever succeed in reaching our goal. On the other hand, instead of thinking of our Ideal afar off, if we think it is manifesting and acting through us, we are able to eliminate all our anxiety and fear of failure. Some people think that by acting the part of our Ideal we grow like our

Ideal. It is very hard for many to do it, for the simple reason that they become conscious of their wants and weaknesses. Many people unconsciously feel their defects when they strive to act the part which they think they are not. The fact that they need to act the part of their Ideal impresses them with the idea of their weaknesses. But when we know, that it is not we, who are acting the part, but the very Ideal itself, it leaves our minds free from all anxiety and thought of false pretension. In our every-day concept we live the life of comparison or relative ideas. We cannot very well shake off the idea of duality all at once. We generally compare two unlike states and conditions. As a result of this comparison we may find one of them is better than the other. If we are conscious that our Ideal is better than we, we cannot wipe out that idea so easily. If we try to force the idea upon our minds that we are that Ideal it may create a kind of contradiction.

Some people are so constituted that they have the simplicity of a child's faith. They can accept any idea without giving much thought to their defects. For the average persons the best road to follow is to surrender themselves to their great Ideal. It takes away the worries and responsibilities of their minds and brings a sense of peace and security. We ought to bear this in mind, that without peace and calmness we cannot manifest our Ideals. It is the one requisite condition we ought to seek first by all means. That does not mean we have to be worried and anxious about it; it simply means we have to adopt such means as will ensure that condition. And it means we have to surrender ourselves to our Great Ideal. When we know that that Ideal is All-health, All-life and the fulfillment of all our desires we cannot help but manifest perfect health and life.

There is a great difference between the Ideal to be reached and the Ideal which is the acting and moving agent in life. One leaves us in the expectation and anticipation, while the other gives us the realization. In striving for the Ideal to be reached we encounter many difficulties. There are moments of discouragement, doubt and fear. Comparatively very few people are seen to reach it through the many trials it presents before them.

In order to succeed in anything we must have the realization of our ability. That is to say, we never succeed in our undertakings without embodying the Ideal which we call ability. Our ability grows with us. But we can never hope to succeed in anything if we are doubtful of our ability. It is not good policy to start to develop our ability with the thought that we have no ability; it keeps our mind pre-occupied, with the consciousness of our inability, which makes our work uninteresting and tedious. The affirmation that "we can" is good and well, provided it has no suggestion to the effect that we can not. But when we affirm we can, not because we can not, but because Almighty God is manifesting through us, then really we can. It is the sense of responsibility and inability which makes our affirmation "we can" null and void. But when we shift our responsibility to our Great Ideal we lose sight of our inability. In fact we do not care whether we have any ability or not. Therefore we notice people who are simple minded and believe in the inspiration from the Lord, display a remarkable degree of power and efficiency in their work which they trustingly undertake to do. These people may not always do things rationally, but what they do, they do with power and efficiency. They being ignorant of the law, may attribute everything to the work of the Lord. But who can question for a moment, that they draw their inspiration from the Great Cosmic power by their simple trust? Some people may doubt it on the ground that many of their actions are so inconsistent, that there cannot be any relation to the Cosmic power. But if they think for a moment that the Cosmic energy is above good and bad, and consistency and inconsistency, and it acts in the direction of least resistance, they will have no reason to doubt it. The simple trust in one's self or in the Almighty God will bring a person in touch with the Cosmic energy, and will make it flow through his being, according to his mental concept and capacity. Having been born and raised in the environment of imperfect concept, very few people can have absolute trust in themselves. Only by trusting in their perfect Ideal according to their concept can they overcome the concept of their environment. Then again, Cosmic energy manifests itself without any qualification such as good and bad. We interpret it good or bad according to our concept. Our concept changes with the realization of our higher Ideal. For example, many so called just actions of our ancestors may be considered unjust by us. Similarly, many of our actions may be viewed critically by our posterity. Cosmic energy always manifests just in exact proportion and quality of our concept. The higher the concept, the greater is the manifestation of Cosmic energy. By limiting our concept of life we limit the manifestation of Cosmic energy. When a man knows his Divine rights he is never satisfied remaining a limitation, or in a state of stagnation. Stagnated mind harbors fear on account of its limited knowledge of self. By surrendering itself to a higher Ideal it can be free from all fear and limitation. Fear may not be always conquered by the affirmation of courage. But we can always conquer it by trusting ourselves in the hands of the Great Ideal. The scriptures say, resist no evil. We may add just as well, fight no fear, no anger, and passion; surrender everything to the Lord God, your Ideal. Your fear, anger, passion, will be transmuted into the quality or concept of your Ideal. It is not the destruction of our individuality but the expansion of it. It is by giving the smaller life, we receive the greater one. That is what the Master meant when He said: "He that loseth his life for My sake shall find it." Let anyone lose his life for the sake of his highest Ideal he will find it again in that Ideal. Master Jesus became God by giving up His flesh-self, or limited self, to God. Thus He showed us an example of salvation from the limited concept of life. He is to-day our Life and the way. The name of that Life is, "I and my Father are one." He is the way because He showed us how to have perfect unity with God.

III

Before we can come into our full realization we must recognize our Divine right to demand or ask. Jesus said: "For everyone that asketh receiveth; and he that seeketh findeth; and to him that knocketh it shall be opened." What shall we demand first? The Master said: "Seek ye first the kingdom of God and His righteousness, and all these things shall be added unto you." Where is the kingdom of God? Within. What is the condition of the kingdom of God? Abiding trust, calmness and peace. When we enter into the kingdom of God we come face to face with God. That is to say, when we find calmness and peace within ourselves we come in touch with the Cosmic Life. Then, and then alone, we receive the fresh life current which clears away the stagnant condition of our being, which is due to our limited concept of Life. Then we come to the realization that all that we desire is in God. And we being in God and living in the vitalizing current of Life are able to draw whatever we want. Life and health are abundant for us and also for those who want to receive from us. Then anyone receiving from us receives from God; because we cease to exist as man of flesh. When Almighty God manifests to us we become such medium as God alone can use.

Many people not knowing the law, when in want become anxious to get the object they want. Had they understood the injunction of the Master they would have first sought the kingdom of God. When we find the kingdom of God, that is, calmness and peace, we receive the inspiration or the direction how to get our desired object. When we keep our mind on the object we want, and not the means whereby the object can be had, we fail to receive it. Therefore let us not forget that the Cosmic law of supply always works through us, when we are calm and peaceful, after we have made the demand in perfect trust. Whenever we carry our desires to the Heaven of peace and calmness, Almighty God fulfills our desires. It is the Law of the creation, which the God-loving soul alone is able to understand. They say that the Cosmic consciousness, as ignorantly nowadays we call sub-conscious mind, acts better through us during our sleep. The only thing we are supposed to do, is to carry our desire or suggestion over to sleep. It is not the sleep, but the calmness and peace within us, which facilitate the action of the sub-conscious. We cannot reach our sub-conscious with our desire or suggestion if we go to sleep with anxiety and restlessness. But then if anyone has faith in the working of the sub-conscious, his case may be an exception to the rule.

The very fact that one has faith ensures a certain amount of peace and calmness. Faith is the great moral agent to inspire confidence and to ensure peace and contentment. We can reach the sub-conscious or Cosmic consciousness any time if we can be calm and peaceful. But sleep being considered the natural state of calmness and peace, some people lay special stress on it. We know from our experiences that sleep is not always the indication of calmness and peace. Children seem to sleep soundly, on account of their care-free minds. From this fact it is supposed that we can easily reach their sub-conscious with suggestions.

The Master says: "All things whatsoever we shall ask in prayer, believing, ye shall receive." Prayer means the understanding of our relation with God. Belief means the trust which gives us that calm assurance. According to the Master, when we understand our relation with God, whenever we ask anything with calmness and peace, we receive it.

The simple trust in our Ideal gives us an amount of spiritual uplift we never gain by affirmation for power and strength, as we never feel quite free from suggestion or consciousness of our weakness. From our very childhood we have been trained to accept two opposites, such as good and bad, strength and weakness, health and disease. It is so simple, yet it may sound strange to us that one of these opposites suggest the other. When we speak about strength we mean that it is opposite to weakness and vice versa.

If we are conscious of the fact that we affirm for strength because we are weak, we can hardly have the full benefit of our affirmation. Not knowing any other way to overcome our early suggestions of polar opposites, we resort to a means which is vastly superior to anything in the line of suggestion. It is to give ourselves to our Ideal and to let that Ideal manifest through us unhindered.

If thought is a living force, then feeling is being. In fact we live in the feeling. Feeling is the only reality in the human sense. If our feeling or the condition of our being manifests externally through our personality and affects those around us, why will not our feeling of God-power manifest through us and affect others? We can feel any condition by imagination. There is no harm then to imagine that God-power is flowing through us. As the stagnant water is re-vitalized by the fresh contact of running water, our whole system is similarly revived into full life by the contact of Cosmic Life. The imagination regarding the manifestation of our Ideal through our being will in time bring us the realization. Effectiveness of a suggestion is more due to our imagination than certain fixed affirmations. While affirmations have a certain chance to arouse opposition, the imagination has none. It is a mental picture in progression without any interruption from opposing suggestion. Suppose it has its opposing suggestion; even then it is more fruitful when applied to our Ideal than anything else. Christian Yoga teaches that there is no need of denying or affirming the disease or condition we want to be rid of. Simply come into the realization by imagination that Divine Life abundant is flowing through you, and your whole being is undergoing transformation. We need not think,

24

whether we are healthy or sick. The only thought we ought to think is, that God is All-health and All-good, and we live, move and have our being in Him. Since God-Life is the only life and our life is the part manifestation of that life, it is our Divine heritage to manifest as much God-life as we want to.

If we think something is the matter with us, we ought to immediately know that our nature or inner unfoldment is giving us warning to manifest more God-life. Disease really means lack of ease. When we are not comfortable with the amount of life and condition we are manifesting it is a sure sign that stagnation has been caused in our being. Since our concept is our being, we can right the defect by changing our concept for better. No concept can be better than the concept that the Almighty God is manifesting through us, or the God-life is flowing through us. We ought to always remember that disease is not a power but a condition. The condition which may affect one may not affect another. Therefore disease is not a fixed condition. Our individuality is determined by our concept or understanding. As our concept changes, so changes our individuality. Hence our individuality is not a fixed entity, but a conditional state. According to our state or condition of being we feel easy or uneasy. If the demand of this state is well supplied we feel easy and to the contrary, we feel the reverse. The name of that demand is more life. Whenever any part of the body is afflicted we ought to immediately know that that part lacks the proper amount of life, or demands a certain amount of life according to its natural state, which we call constitution. Really there is nothing natural or unnatural in our being. What may be natural to-day may not be considered so to-morrow. By the word natural we mean a state which agrees with and corresponds to our being or concept. When any part is afflicted in the sense of the world we at once know that part does not agree with our being. We never consider a disease a part affliction since it can not manifest without affecting our whole being or concept. Whenever any disease manifests through any part of the body we know something is the matter with our concept. Our concept needs growth and expansion; in other words, it needs more life. Generally our concept -is formed by the impressions we receive every day. With our growth and unfoldment we come to a stage where we can change our concept by self-impressions. Sometimes we cling to an old concept, though we have received many new impressions to form a new concept. That is the time the law of our being demands that we must have a new life. Many people have cured their ailments by changing their concept of life. No matter what your concept of life, you have always room for improvement. Since our concept is our life, let the concept of God-life occupy our mind. It will always fill our being with God-life to the brim of its capacity. As by the exercise we develop our strength, so by exercise we develop our capacity. The more God-life we draw unto us the more capacity we develop.

Though some people are not living spiritual lives according to our standard, yet they seem to enjoy good health. They may seem to many as a living protest to this teaching. But when we understand the law we easily find the solution. Each individual, as it is stated before, is his concept, and this concept needs change according to the demand created within him by the law of creation or being. Whenever we create consciously or unconsciously conditions which call for better concept we must make the change or we will bring suffering on ourselves. The man who does not live his own life which belongs to him by his Divine rights of being is a hypocrite. The man who is a hypocrite against the protest of his own being or concept commits sin against the Holy Ghost. The Ghost which is our rightful soul, or being, or concept is ever holy. It is our conscience or the better understanding. We must live according to our better understanding, if we want to be free from sin or the limited concept. As long as we are moving towards the Infinite Life so long we are free from

26

sin. The spiritual concept of some people is very crude. Their progress towards the spiritual concept of life may seem to us very slow and we may think they are hopelessly lost in gross materialism, but nevertheless they are coming to the better understanding of life. If their minds and bodies are healthy it is because they are living their life according to their concept, and they are changing their concept according to the demands of their being. No man ever can have a healthy mind and body sinning against his nature.

A man who has not a healthy mind cannot have a healthy body. All healthy looking people are not always healthy. Some people living a wrong life, as we use the term in the relative sense, seem to suffer from no reaction or retribution, but they are sooner or later brought to the understanding of the law of life. Reward and punishment are the simple operation of the law of our being. In reality there is no difference between them, except the interpretation we put to the law of causation or compensation. We gain in either case, through reward and punishment. Both are for our better understanding of life. The law of causation or of cause and effect is the law of our being. In this relative plane of good and bad, every action according to our interpretation works some change in our being by the re-action which we call effect. This change always brings us to the better understanding of the law of our being. In many cases it may not be noticeable externally, but internally that change is going on just the same. Suffering which we call punishment is always caused by our neglect to give response to the demand of our being. When we require more life or a greater concept of life we must not fail to give response to that demand if we want to avoid suffering. The right or wrong interpretation makes our suffering either a blessing or a curse. We ought to understand this, that suffering is not punishment inflicted by God Almighty, but it is a natural process through which we are brought to the better understanding or consciousness of our being. By the neglect of giving response to the universal demand of ourself or the

27

better understanding, we create around us a shell or a cover as it were. It requires extra effort to break through this shell in order to reach the proper condition by the law of life. In this ever progressive universe we cannot remain long in our old condition, the condition which we must pass by the law of our being. That condition of sin or the concept of undue limitation is bound to end. Sinful life is always lost in the ocean of Divine consciousness through many sufferings.

IV

We maintain our first assertion all through our metaphysics that there is no misery, disease or death, except what our thinking makes for us. The same thing can be said about health, happiness and immortality. This simply goes to prove that in this relative plane, good and bad, health and disease, happiness and unhappiness are only the results of our thinking. This simple statement alone cannot undo the things which our thoughts have already wrought for us. It may require time for any one to contract the habit of disease thoughts, since health is the natural state of our being. In the cultivation of a taste for morbid mental condition is found much of the misery and wretchedness of humanity. Yet there is an undercurrent of something in us which is wholesome and pure. These thoughts of health and disease, happiness and misery, immortality and death, indicate nothing but the duality of concept. This concept invites one or the other of the polar opposites. In this world of God the polar opposites cannot exist in reality. They exist only in our thoughts. Hence our thoughts, which create them, are in error in the absolute sense. These polar opposites are our mental illusion, that is, they exist in our thought or belief, but in the absolute sense they do not exist. Whatever we believe to have existence, the same relatively exists to us. A thing or a condition which is unreal to others we can make real to us by constant thought. In this relative plane everything exists as we think of it. Sometimes some thing exists, but we see it according to the nature of the thought of it; sometimes some thing does not exist, but we make its existence possible by our thought. In either case, in the form we see a thing, it is real to us. In this relative plane everything is real if our thinking makes it so. An imaginary trouble is as real to the sufferer as the real one. Hence reality and unreality are simply matters of selection by thought, or recognition by thought. These illusions of polar opposites are due to our thought. Since they are opposite to the great fundamental principle of creation they stand in our way to salvation or perfect understanding of the truth. A thing or condition which is less than the other is not opposite to it. Hence the disease which means less health or life is not an opposite condition to health. If we want to understand the great principle of our being we ought to free ourselves from this illusion of polar opposites. It is this illusion which makes the suggestive science impracticable, and which keeps us from the perfect unity with God. The less conscious we are of a polar opposite of an affirmation the greater will be the effect of the affirmation. According to the new psychology we impress our sub-conscious mind with a thought or an idea which we are conscious of. Now if our affirmation of a certain condition makes us conscious of its opposite, our sub-conscious will be impressed with that of which it is conscious. Especially if our affirmation bears any suggestion to the condition which our sub-conscious already has, it will impress the sub-conscious more with that which it has. We are told to be careful not to permit opposite thought to come to our mind when we affirm for a certain condition or thing. But we are not told how we can overcome the suggestion of polar opposites. We admit that some people, owing to the simplicity of faith or strong concentration, can easily forget the opposite of an affirmation. It will be very hard for the average self-conscious person to do it. Christian Yoga, however, shows us a way which is very easy to follow and which is the safest of all. It is not to take any thought of our strength or weaknesses, but to give ourselves to our perfect Ideal, and to let that Ideal manifest through us. It is the grandest truth in the world; only those that are spiritually inclined will understand it. If from the force of habit any thought of duality of concept comes to your mind, at once come to the understanding by discrimination that less is not opposite to more and that more is the legitimate demand of our being, because growth or expansion is the natural law of our being. Now the question is whether the attributes, All-health, All-good, suggest their polar opposites. We ought to remember that when we use those attributes we use them in the absolute sense. There can not exist any condition beyond the Absolute to compare with it. The less health, which we call disease, is also a part of the All-health. The Cosmic Life is really beyond all attributes. Because whenever we give any attribute to anything, we suggest its relative condition. Yet living in this relative plane we are to fight the battle of relative conditions by relative suggestions. When we say the relative conditions, we do not mean the conditions of polar opposites, but we simply mean conditions which merely suggest comparison, such as more and less. At the same time we do not forget the fact that more and less are both less than the most. Yet it is in the most that more and less exist. They really do not exist in the absolute sense, but they do exist in the relative sense. When we take the Absolute as parts we try to find it in the parts, or in the relative. The Absolute, being All-in-All, we find It also in Its parts. But it can never be its parts. It is ever whole without any change. We only think it to be a part by our part realization. The Absolute as a part exists only in our concept. That which changes cannot be the Absolute. That is to say, the Absolute never changes. But its parts seem to change on account of their existing in our concept. Since our concept changes regarding the Absolute, our concept of it is anything but a perfect concept. As by seeing a part of a machine in operation one may think it is the whole machine in operation, so by the part realization one may think it is the Absolute. Or one may have the idea that a part acts independent of the whole. Either concept is far from truth in the absolute sense. As we never call a machine by its component parts, so we never call the Absolute by its parts. Even in the relative sense we never call any member of our body man, though we know it is a part of man. As far as the movement of that particular organ is concerned it is distinct from the rest. But whether it is the movement of one or more organs it is nevertheless the action of the whole man. So in every thing we see the working of the one Divine Intelligence as a whole, though according to our interpretation or concept it is taking on different colors. We can here use the crude illustration of colored glasses and sunlight. As the sunlight passing through different colored glasses seemingly partakes of the colors of them, so divine consciousness apparently partakes of the nature of our concepts. These concepts are ever changeable. Our thought, right or wrong in the relative sense, gives birth to our concept. Our concept being relative the thought which gives birth to it is also relative. Anything relative is nonpermanent and unreal in the absolute sense. By rising above the relative, or the duality of concept we become free from the illusion. By thinking of this illusion we can never be free from it. The only thing we can do is to forget all about ourselves and our past and think of the Great Universal Ideal. Remember, that nothing can free us from the bondage of illusion except that which is above all illusion.

Some people want to be happy by seeking material means. From the testimonies of the world, they ought to know that seeking happiness in this material world by material means is like trying to find water in a mirage. The material world, or the world of limited concept, cannot give us the happiness which belongs to the spiritual world. This material world becomes spiritual by our concept. It is an unrealized truth to many that by our thought we can transform material things into spiritual. When we see Almighty God in everything and every action we forget that the so-called material world exists at all. This material world which exists only in our concept vanishes from our sight with the change of our concept. Then we see everything in a different light. And then we come to know that things are not what they seem. When the same thing looks different to us, it loses its identity. When the material things become spiritual we do not know them the same any longer. That is why, when we wake up as it were, to see the whole universe before us pulsating with life, we lose the identity of the inanimate material world. What a grand awakening that is! It means the undoing of the whole of our creation. Then we come to know that our creation and God's creation are vastly different from each other. We create our world by thought or imagination, according to our concept, and Almighty God creates His by His being. One is a lifeless, unstable creation and the other is eternal and permanent. Men and women, animals, vegetables and minerals rest in that one grand Symbol called eternal life. Our life, being merely our concept, symbolizes but a dead stream of a mighty ocean. Standing on the heights of great spiritual concept of life, when we look around us we perceive but a vast ocean of Divine life. When a man loses himself in God-consciousness he forgets his own past. He forgets everything pertaining to time and space. He discovers that the whole dictionary is full of misapplied words, words which are all empty and meaningless. The material man gives names to things, which never exist except in his thought. The things as we see and understand them never exist in the reality. We see them according to our concept. When we come to know that a man and a tree mean the same thing to us, then we call them by one common name. The Divine intelligence and life in the man and the tree is always one and the same. When we live in that life we forget all names which are the marks of differentiation in our temporal creation. These things around us may stand to others just the same, but to those who have great awakening they will vanish in their particular significance.

32

The man who is in illusion or in limitation does not know any difference from that which appeals to his limited concept. Everything he sees is real to him. Everything appears to him according to the value he puts upon it. According to its value a thing reacts upon our mind. In fact we recognize a thing by its reaction or impression. There is no difference between a five dollar gold piece and a nickel. The only difference between them is the value we put upon them. It makes the two objects look different in significance. They react upon us according to the value we put upon them. Now if the value is the real significance of a thing, it does not exist apart from that value. If its existence does not cause any reaction on our mind it makes no difference whether it exists or not. We admit the existence of a thing when we are conscious of it. Whenever we are conscious of a thing it reacts upon our mind according to its value, or the reaction of a thing upon our mind makes us conscious of it. It is the relationship which we establish with the world by creating an artificial value that affects our whole being and allures us to stay in bondage. The master minds of the east say that it is through the attachment we create illusion. When we cease to attach any artificial or unreal value to the things around us we become free from all pain and misery. In order to know any two things we differentiate their relative values which give birth to our relative concept. Suppose we forget the relative value or significance of all things existing in space and time, it is doubtful whether we can know them at all. No word, no thought, no condition ever can affect us if we do not take them in the value which concerns us. What affects us are not the things or the conditions, but our own concept regarding them. The concept which affects us is called illusion by the wise men. This world of pain, misery, worry and death is the world of false creation or illusion. The master minds of the east came to the realization of that fact many thousands of years ago. Master Jesus referred to the same thing in parables and stories.

To-day after the lapse of many centuries we have the same revelation. In order to stop our pain, misery and death we must stop our false creation in order to attain to that state, which Lord Buddha called Nirvana. Nirvana means the cessation of the creation of lower desires or of the false concept of things and conditions. When we attain to Nirvana we live in the God consciousness. Then living in this so-called visible world we live not, and acting in this world we act not. Whatever is done is done by the Almighty God. We simply live, move and have our being in Him. Then God's action will be interpreted by the material man as our action. Oh! what a grand life this is! Only those who are awakened will understand the deep mystery of this life. But those who are still in slumber, under the cover of illusion, will not hear the voice of the Almighty. Even if they hear, they will not understand. Either their false pride or ignorance will keep them away from the blissful life. When a man has the right concept of life he worships his God in true spirit. He knows that one grand universal concept comprises all. That grand awakening of which we are speaking comes gradually and slowly. At first a man realizes the consciousness in every thing. This consciousness is reciprocal. He finds himself exchanging his thought of better understanding of life with the things around him. Gradually he comes to the realization of the consciousness even in the space. Then he is initiated in the mystic universal language which is only spoken by soul, and which is without word. That grand symbolical language we understand by feeling. It is so silent yet so expressive that when we feel it there remains no doubt or misunderstanding regarding the truth it speaks. When once we are initiated into that language we understand the message of trees, flowers, rocks, sun, moon and the stars. It is not poetic sentiment as some people are liable to say, but it is a grand truth, vital reality. We cannot make anyone understand it, if

34

he himself does not try to understand it. We ought not to be over-anxious to induce anyone to follow this line of thought. We know everyone is coming this way consciously or unconsciously. If we understand this truth then let us spread it broadcast. It is the command of the Almighty God or the Great Law of our being that we should bear the message of truth to every land and every clime. The truth is open and eternal, and it is for all. We ought to remember what the Master said, "For verily I say unto you, that many prophets and righteous men have desired to see those things which ye see and have not seen them; and to hear those things which ye hear, and have not heard them."

Whether the truth is accepted or rejected we ought not to lose our poise and calmness. Whenever we lose our mental poise, no matter how great or trivial is the cause, we detach ourselves from the truth. The joy which comes to those who obey the mandate of their higher self has no comparison. When the man obeys and follows the lead of his higher concept he does his duty. If he wants to realize still higher concept he ought not to do anything else. The Almighty law of supply always knows what is his want and it gives ready response to his innermost desires. Men with the greater concept of life do their duty according to their inner prompting and leave everything in the hand of Providence. It is a great relief to know that we can trust our cares and burdens to the Great law of life. The man who knows God and follows Him never knows what is want. God never fails us if we can have absolute trust in Him. When we know that the kingdom of God is within us we are able to free ourselves from our cares. Here within ourselves whatever we seek we find. The fountainhead of all supply is there. The new psychology tells us that it is the sub-conscious plane, and once we can reach that plane without desires or thoughts we find ready response from it. The sub-conscious mind or Almighty God dwells within us. We can find God any time by retiring within ourselves. What does the word within mean? It means a condition unruffled by the external world. The external world which is our own creation is constantly reacting upon us with the thoughts and ideas which we are sending forth. When we stop this reaction from our every day thought-creation of sense desires we reach the within. Then in that stillness of unruffled consciousness we receive inspiration direct from God. Without the proper understanding of ourselves we cannot enter into the Kingdom of God. The Kingdom of God is so near yet so far. A little change of concept makes a lot of difference. In the plane of idea or thought we travel thousands of miles in a second. The distance between two ideas may be millions of miles, yet it takes but a second to change from one idea to another. So many people not knowing about the thought world maintain that our thought travels through the space. Space there is none in that subtle plane of consciousness. But looking from the limited concept of life we are liable to think that communication between the two thought-entities is conducted through the space. If any two persons receive the same idea at the same time through their minds we account for it by telepathic relation. But we forget to take note of the fact that if any two persons receive an idea at the same time from an unknown source it is not due to transmission but absorbtion or realization. In one great indivisible consciousness we live, move and have our being. Our consciousness is the part expression of that omnipresent consciousness. There is no detachment or break in that Cosmic Consciousness. If we consider ourselves limited, it is because of our limited concept of life. That concept exists only in our thought, and with the change of thought that concept changes, and vice versa. Consequently a changeable thing cannot change that which is unchangeable. In reality there is no limitation or cessation in Consciousness. If this world is the world of Consciousness there cannot exist any other medium except that. Since we reach our own consciousness by absorbing the higher idea, we receive by absorbtion or realization all the ideas and thoughts which in the absolute sense

36

are ours, but in the relative sense others. In the Absolute we exist whether in reality or in the concept. Consequently nothing can be realized by us which is not in the Absolute. The relative existence is but the conditional existence and the Absolute is the only real existence. Between two relative existences we see nothing but two relative conditions. What we call transmission of thoughts and ideas is the absorbtion or realization of conditions. One is absorbing the conditions of the other, thereby he is coming to realize all that there is in that condition. The temporary absorbtion of conditions is called telepathy. Then if a message comes to us through so-called space it is because of our concept. In the Absolute there is no space or time. Space and time are the relative conditions. They do not exist apart from our limited concept. The people who are living in the material plane will not be able to comprehend this truth. Only those who have the great spiritual awakening will understand it by absorbtion or intuition, but not by reason. If any one wants to receive illumination of the divine wisdom let him give himself up to the Great Fountainhead of all knowledge.

When we realize a condition, we become that in the subjective sense. We, ourselves, are nothing but conditions. These conditions hold our relative existence. These conditions or our thought-creations are at first subjective in the relative sense. They mark our individuality. They are constantly changing from subjective to objective forms. The objective or visible forms are as much thought forms as that of the subjective. One is only more concentrated expression than the other. When we say concentrated expression we do not use the term in the literal sense. We use it in the sense of a metaphor. It simply means a condition well defined or well formed. Whenever an inner condition is well defined it approaches near to the objective expression. Then if we see it, it is not because it is less subtle than the subjective form, but because it is more well defined. To use the illustration of an object beyond our sight, at first we do not see it. As it gradually approaches nearer to our vision we see it, but not distinctly. When it is very near to our sight we see it very clearly and in every detail. So a condition which is far from our concept does not manifest through us. But when it becomes a part of our being through realization we express it in the objective or the so-called visible form. Whenever we realize any condition, no matter what it is, we show it in our external appearance. We may use all the art to conceal it from the critical observers, but it is in vain. That indefinable stamp of the inner condition can be observed in our faces and features. Hence there is a reason to believe that all forms are the outward expressions of certain inner conditions. These conditions may be in us or in the things which represent certain forms. Sometimes we see forms which exist only in our mind or in us. These forms we generally call illusory. But as far as the reality of forms is concerned there is no difference between the illusory and the so-called real forms except in the point of duration. We can take the illustration of the forms which appear in our dreams. All the forms in dreams produce the same feeling in us as they do in our waking state. Only these forms exist in more temporary conditions than those of the waking state. Even in the waking state we see more or less temporary forms. One will always exist to our consciousness so long as we remain in this limited concept of life, and another is the temporary reproduction of our own mental condition. As far as we are concerned all forms exist in our relative plane or in our concept. So we can just as well say that all forms exist in us. We exist in the Absolute, and the Absolute exists in us. Therefore all that exists in us also exists in the Absolute. And now we can reverse the statement and say that all that exists in the Absolute also exists in us. We, as an individual, exist by our concept, that is, we exist as we think ourselves to be. Since we change ourselves by changing our thought in regard to ourselves, we have no permanent existence. Therefore our existence is mortal in the relative sense. Then if we are not what we think ourselves to be, we must be something that we are not in the relative sense. Nothing can be so self-evident as the assertion of one's own existence. Even though we may assert something that we are not, yet we are always something which we do not assert ourselves to be. Even in a false declaration we find a declarer, who stands apart from his declaration. It is very easy to understand that a declarer and his declaration are not the same. This declarer must be more than his concept. Let us take the illustration of an arch in space. What do we see when we see an arch? We see the space temporarily defined by some material which has given the space a form. This form cannot possibly be of the material which has been used to form the arch, since all forms are the space described. It cannot be space either, since space is beyond all forms. Then whence comes the form of the arch? It is simply an apparent condition of the space which has no relation to it in reality. So that something, which declares or asserts is not the thing or condition asserted. For example, if a beggar asserts that he is a king, it does not change his condition. Hence the subject who asserts is not changed by its assertion, if that assertion is opposed or contrary to its nature. As a part cannot be its whole so the immortal cannot be mortal even by declaration. The concept which changes does not change that which is the root of all concept. As a part view of a picture is not the whole picture so our concept is not the Absolute. As gradually removing the cover from the picture we change the already exposed part, so gradually taking away the veil of ignorance we change our lower concept.

Now the question is, whether the subject or the immortal principle can make such assertion as will contradict its own nature. If we judge the whole problem from the standpoint of the Absolute we can easily find the solution. The Absolute is beyond all time, space and condition. Therefore its action cannot be bound by time. Yet without time we cannot think of any action. In order to act we must start from a certain point of time and stop at a certain other point. Consequently there is always a past and future to our action. We can never act in the present, since the duration of time which we call present is really past. Present tense cannot exist in the relative plane. The Absolute alone can exist in the present. Now if we say that the Absolute acts we cannot conceive its action other than its being. As the sun and its rays are inseparable so the Absolute and its action are inseparable. The act of living is as much of an act as the act of doing. In this sense nothing can exist without its action. Since nothing really exists besides the Absolute, there cannot be any other actor. We do not exist except as the part of the Absolute. Hence we act too. When a part judges the action of the whole its judgment is always at fault. Since the part's action is the part action of the whole, its conception of its own action may be wrong. There is nothing apparent in the world of God. What is, always is. What does not exist cannot exist. In reality this relative plane does not exist, therefore there cannot be any question that the subject, the immortal essence can really have relative experiences. Leaving aside this philosophical discourse, if we face the problem of life as we find it, we solve it in a different manner. We know that our life is what we believe it to be. Even here we maintain our assertion that in reality there is no sin, misery or death. But if anyone believes their existence they exist to him. In this existence of belief, or thought-life, we try to solve a problem according to our concept.

VI

One thing we are bound to admit, namely, that there is nothing stationary or unchangeable in this life or thought or concept. Yet in most cases we are responsible for the change we undergo. Change is inevitable in this transitory world, but we can make that change to suit ourselves. If that change brings us sin, misery and death we are bound to accept them according to the law of preference. We can regulate the change in the way we want to. Some people take sin, misery and death as settled conditions, therefore they find them in every action, according to their interpretation. We interpret an action according to our concept. Consequently our concept and the interpretation of an action correspond to each other. The same action according to our interpretation reacts on us differently. So the difference between hell and heaven is the difference of their interpretation, according to our concept. Now the question is, how are we to change our concept at will,?

We know whenever we consciously put forth effort to change it, we are overwhelmed by the enormity of the task, and we become so self-conscious that our effort challenges the very condition we want to get rid of. The solution of this problem is very simple. We are to trust in our Great Ideal. When we shift all our responsibilities to our Great Ideal, God, we are ever free from the reaction of our past concept. God as he is, we know not. We know him as we think him to be. If we can ever surrender ourselves to our highest and best Ideal we will have nothing to worry us. Then if we live, we live not for ourselves, but we live for our Ideal. We never feel the burden of cares of the world and the strain of our work. When our mind is peaceful and our nerves are quiet we are able to manifest superhuman power and energy. In fact, we manifest as much power as we realize our Ideal to possess. Because we cease to exist and our Ideal lives through us. What wonders our concept can work! No psychology or philosophy can show us a better way to the mastery of our self than this simple teaching does. What does psychology or philosophy amount to if it cannot give us a glimpse of the peace which we are all seeking? It is through the path of peace we reach the goal of peace. If we once strike it, all the trials and tribulations of the world cannot lead us astray from the truth. What a grand idea it is to think, that Almighty God is our guide and protector and He is with us always. When that idea inspires our soul to dare and to do, we forget the word fear. Can a man go astray when his soul is filled with the idea of living and acting God? No; it is impossible. If a man goes astray, it is because he counts more upon the ephemeral things than the mandate of his higher self or better understanding. Every step we take toward the fullness of life, we feel the arms of the Almighty around us. We can interpret it either symbolically or literally. The grasp of every new and better idea is the grasp of God.

If we follow his mandate, which is Christ, He will be with us alway, even unto the end of the world, the material concept. Man cannot go alone through the valley of death or material concept. He needs a companion to follow him all the way. Suggestions of mere words are not sufficient to stimulate his mind into hope and courage. Affirmation of the word courage may encourage some people, but in the majority of cases it excites more fear by inducing self-consciousness. Why not then have an Ideal, which will be constantly working through you. This Ideal in time becomes real. When we ourselves become our Ideal, there cannot remain any doubt in our mind regarding its reality. When we feel, live or act a thing it is a reality to us. The reality of our lives depends upon our realization. That realization may be viewed rightly or wrongly by others, but to us it is a real life. Apart from this consciousness of being we have no other evidence to prove our existence. If our realization of certain conditions is our life, it is very easy to be what we want to be. If happiness is our goal we can be happy by realizing or living that condition. The affirmation of the word happiness may stimulate our mind to acquire it, but by feeling that condition we come to the realization. Now the question is, how we can come to feel it. It is by holding the thought, that the Great Happiness is manifesting through us. If we can imagine for a time that it is coming and that we are feeling, we will soon begin to feel it. Then some people are liable to say, that it is not the real happiness, but that it is an imaginary or self-hypnotic condition. Now we should like to ask the question, what is the difference between the two forms of happiness, as far as our feeling is concerned. We live by our feeling of realization of conditions. Apart from that, this life is of no significance to us in this relative plane. Then there cannot be any difference in our feeling of a condition except in degrees. When we come right down to the fact, we are forced to admit, that all our conditions are more or less imaginary. The significance of a so-called real condition depends upon the imaginary value we put upon it. Hence from the beginning to the end we see nothing but the continuous play of imagination. Some people maintain, that apart from the mental plane imagination has very little value. Therefore the psycho-physical conditions may be accounted for as imagination, but the pure and simple physical conditions stand alone in their class without any relation to imagination. It is very hard to discriminate where mind begins and where it ends. But we know that up to a certain point mind and body are interdependent. Within that point mind and body blend so closely together that we cannot separate one from the other. At the same time we notice that the point we have referred to, is not the same in everybody. Then another thing we notice is, that the body can influence mind up to a certain limit, but the mind can control the body, through proper training, without any limit, as experiments have shown.

They say that physical conditions such as hunger, passion, and sensation, are hard to control by the mind. Yet we have known cases where these conditions have been successfully controlled by mind for a certain length of time. From this fact the natural supposition is, that they can be controlled for any length of time. The question, however, under discussion is the question of feeling, which constitutes the reality of our life in this relative plane. Feeling belongs to the mind, whether the cause be mental or physical. If the physical sensation of feeling is the indication of our physical existence then that sensation belongs to the mind. Therefore in sleep when part of our consciousness is withdrawn from the physical we do not have so much physical sensation. It naturally follows, that what we call physical is also a part of the mind. Since nothing physical can exist to us, without physical sensation of some form, we may just as well say, that nothing can exist without the mind or being a part of the mind. Since we exist in mind only, we can change the mental condition by feeling, with the help of imagination. How simple this law of life seems to us, once we understand it. For ages the ancient seers and sages have studied the problem of mind and tried to solve it by reducing it into the objective phenomena. As a result of their experiments they found, that there is very little difference between the real and unreal phenomena. In the Absolute plane, phenomena there are none. In the relative plane, as has been already stated, the reality and unreality of a phenomenon depends upon the testimony of our senses or our concept. If those phenomena which exist long in our concept in the duration of time be called real, then the so-called unreal phenomena cannot be very far from that of the real. Therefore the ancient people of the east classed them in the category of nescience. Whether a phenomenon is an optical delusion or real, it produces the same impression upon our mind for the time being. If we are to ascertain the reality of an object by the reaction it produces in our mind then the object in our optical delusion is real. Anything we can sense by sight, touch, and taste we call an object. Why then cannot a vision in our optical delusion be called an object? This vision of an object we can produce and reproduce in our own minds. The same can be reproduced in another's mind by concentrating its picture upon it. It is simply a question of concentrated will and a receptive condition.

VII

If the influence of one mind upon another is so great, as to change its concept for the time being, why will not the influence of the collective minds of our race change our whole mental concept? When a few civilized men are thrown into contact with uncivilized savages by accident, in a few years they are seen to lose some of their pre-acquired manners and sensibilities. What once seemed to them unnatural now may seem perfectly natural. Our sensibility is a matter of our concept. With the change of our concept we lose it. So we find everything internal and external the production and reproduction of our thought-creation or concept. We have stated before that so-called real objects undergo change with our concept. For example, if a sad accident happens to us in a bright, cheery place, we can never consider that place the same any more. This simply goes to prove, that with the change of our concept, regarding a thing, place or condition we see it changed. So the same object is constantly changing before us, both in its significance and form. A silver dollar which to a child seems large in size and value, will not seem to him the same, when he is grown up. Whenever we meditate upon all these things transpiring around us, we find ourselves introduced into the great philosophy of life. Then we are able to take everything at its real valuation. What can give us the greater grasp of the situation than the thought or idea that we can make or unmake our lives by changing our concept. We know that in this relative plane our lives are what we make them. Yet it is very hard to convey this idea to others by philosophical disquisition. Some things in this life are like axioms, they are self-evident to our perception. It is a waste of time to try to explain them by reason. The only way we know them is by developing discrimination and introspection. If we think calmly and quietly we can at once find the reason why we cannot deny ourselves. In the first place, in order to deny ourselves we must have something which denies. In the second place, without admitting the existence of ourselves we cannot deny ourselves. This is a self-evident fact; yet some people would have us believe that such a fact can be disproved by the reason. We cannot be indifferent to the question either, since everything seems so puzzling in this relative world. As in a dream we ask ourselves, whether we are awake or asleep, so in this life we want to be sure whether we exist. Sometimes everything seems to be so dream-like that we demand a tangible proof of all that we see and also of our own existence. If these things around us are not real, how can we, being the observers, be real. It is a scientific fact that a subject and an object are so closely related with each other, that one cannot exist without the other. If these things around us really do not exist, we also really do not exist. Then it will be foolish to argue about things which do not exist. But if we interpret it in a different way, we can get the meaning out of it. It is this, that we do not exist as we think ourselves to be, but we exist as self-existent, so things as we see them do not exist except as self-existent. There is but one thing self-evident, and that is the Absolute; hence we and the things exist as the Absolute. Then in the Absolute there cannot be any creation, or subject and object. But we are conscious of living in the world of creation; consequently onr denial of this creation will not disprove its existence. We must admit that there is a creation and in this creation we find conditions which are good and bad according to our interpretation. We have already proved that in this relative creation good and bad are not opposite to each other, but one is comparatively better than the other. In this creation, when we lose the God-consciousness we fall from paradise. Then sin, misery and death surround us, that is, we become more limited than our better understanding will naturally permit us. We live in such a dark unenlightened condition where God's grace or the God-consciousness does not enter. We can again regain paradise by using discrimination, God only exists, and we live in Him in order to exist. There is nothing higher than truth and God is that truth. We retire into that truth to live the eternal life. Amen.

We have already stated that our sensibility is the matter of our concept. So are all of our mental faculties. We can develop our faculties by bettering our concept. It is a very hard and laborious process to develop our faculties by direct conscious effort. According to the old school we have to go through long and tedious training in order to accomplish the result. But our Yoga science shows us a method to develop our inner faculties, which is very simple and effective. Whenever we want anything, we first ought to understand the law, which supplies all of our demands. The Great All-knowing Consciousness, as we use the term in the relative sense, is within us. We simply go to Him whenever we want anything or want anything done. It does not take very long before we get all that we desire. You may take this literally if you want to, that we can go direct to God to make our personal demand. Why my friend, we can go to God in the same sense as we go to any person. No matter how near a person may be to us if we are not conscious of his presence he does not exist to our consciousness, because we do not get any mental reaction from him, which we call recognition of one's presence. When we approach a thing, if we are not conscious of its nearness, we are just as far away from it. So in this symbolical world space exists only in our concept. The measure which we take of the space is an imaginary measure. We feel the distance of space according to our concept. As our concept changes so changes our concept of space. Before the railroad was introduced New York was to us a great distance from San Francisco, but now it is only a few days' journey. Our space conception regarding the distance between New York and San Francisco has undergone a change. So also it is true of this earth. The people of different countries now feel neighborly to one another, no matter how many thousands of miles may lie between them. We ascertain the nearness or distance of an object by our consciousness of the relative position we occupy. When we are conscious that the Omnipresent God is within us, that is, in our calm unruffled condition of mind, we feel Him near us. Just be conscious that you are in the ocean of Omnipresent Consciousness and you will approach God. It is the simplest thing on earth, yet it is the hardest thing to those who have not the proper understanding. When our concept of God is far, He is far from us, and when near He is near us.

47

Some people not knowing this maintain that the Great illumination comes from above. If they use the word above not in the sense of space but as a figure of speech we agree with them. In reality this Consciousness has nothing to do with the space. It is simply to know something which knows all. In this relative plane nothing is so powerful an agent to bring about change in us as the imagination. We have to imagine a condition or a thing, in order to get it. The condition and thing have no special qualities to satisify our desires. It is our own qualities attributed to them, that reflect back on us. When we receive the thing we desire, we receive the imaginary value of it, which exists only in our mind. It will have no effect on us if we do not give any value to it. Giving value or attribute to a thing means imagining a value regarding it. We desire the value we give to an object, not the object. But for the reason we cannot separate one from the other, we desire the object on account of its value. Hence all desires regarding things are imaginary. We can gain as much satisfaction from imaginary objects as from anything else. For example, an ignorant man may be happy with a piece of brass which he believes to be gold. He may be disappointed if he is informed about his mistake. Notwithstanding the fact it goes to prove that the generally accepted value of a thing is as much of an imaginary value as anything in this world. If the community or society in which we are living puts an artificial value on a thing, in a short time that value becomes real to us. The currency notes issued to meet the emergency are the best example for it. If an imaginary thing or condition produces the same reaction in our mind as would a so-called real thing or condition, we do not see the reason why it would not meet the requirement of our inner desire. So the wise men of the east say that all our desires and their objects are imaginary as far as their values are concerned. Of course we admit that the concept which has stronger and longer hold upon us will always influence us.

VIII

As far as happiness and misery are concerned they are both based on imagination. As it has been already stated that the reality of this life is its realization or feeling, so happiness and misery are a matter of feeling. Our feeling depends upon the imaginary value we attribute to things and conditions. In order to live the greater life we must feel it. We must draw that life to us by the imagination.

In the Absolute or the soul plane there is no need of drawing any thing or condition. Because here all things and conditions sink in the ocean of the universal Consciousness. In fact they do not exist any more. Figuratively speaking as a small light is submerged by a larger light, so these things and conditions lose their existence in the great Universal life. Metaphysically speaking no thing or condition can exist in the Absolute, since it is the only existant. If the imagination is unreal then the conditions and things imagined are also unreal. Then there cannot be any condition called the God Consciousness. The self-existant Absolute does not require any attributes or qualifications. But we know in this relative plane whether a thing or a condition is real or unreal. It is always real to us when we think it so. Because according to our thought regarding a thing or a condition it reacts upon us. This reaction makes our lives as we find them. Then our thought regarding the greater consciousness ought to react on us and mould our lives accordingly. We want the greater consciousness, because we are not satisfied with our smaller consciousness. Our consciousness of which we are conscious is our concept. No matter how unreal this concept may be, it is the sum total of the impressions we have received from the things and conditions, according to the imaginary values put upon them. Similarly, by forming the impressions of the greater consciousness we can have the greater concept. The value which we put upon our consciousness makes it small or great. Since all values are imaginary, we can reach the greater consciousness by putting an imaginary value upon it. It is not the denial of the existence of God, as some superficial readers may think, but it is the admittance of a God who is above all relative conditions. The God with attributes whom we worship is the God of our concept, therefore He is not the Absolute. Whenever we give any attribute to any thing we limit it, in other words we drag it down to the relative plane or the plane of comparison. But as we use a thorn to take out another thorn in our finger, so we destroy one relative concept with another. When our purpose is served we do not want any of them. Now we know how to reach God. Demanding anything of God is to believe that God has it. Whatever God has we have too by the reason of our being a part of Him. When we say God we mean God as we understand Him in His relative plane. Our relative concept of God corresponds to our nature. We cannot imagine our God to be more than our mental capacity or our concept permits us. In this sense we are making our own God. Even in this making, the eternal truth exists. Whatever might be our concept, our real self exists as eternal, indestructible principle. But in this relative plane we become what we want to be. The same thing is true of our demand, we get what we want. It has been already stated that we are part of God, that is, part of our highest Ideal. We are not that Ideal, but we bear a close relation to it. In this relative world everything, thinking makes and unmakes. If we can really think that we have a thing, we have it. But the suggestion of the polar opposites is so strong, we cannot hold that thought without having the adverse suggestion, but the thought that our Ideal has it and we have a right to share it as part of that Ideal, has no adverse suggestion. Whatever belongs to the whole belongs also to the part. When we think or believe that our Ideal has the thing we want, It really has. Because our thinking makes everything. In this sense we make ourselves, we make our Ideal, and we make the thing we want. It is always so in this relative creation. Where all creation stops we join

50

there with the Absolute, the eternal self-existant Principle which never changes. Whenever we think of anything with a certain attribute, it partakes of the nature of the attribute. In reality it is nothing but what we think it to be. Because what we think of a thing, the same reacts on us. When we think of a condition in such a degree, that we really come to believe in its existence, it becomes a living entity. When we believe that we have taken poison, though we have not, we feel the effect of it just the same. So if we believe in the magic power of a stick it has decided influence over us. The savage by giving all the higher attributes of God to a piece of stone has all the sufferings and reward from it. Seeing this creative power in man, some people are liable to think that man is the only God in this creation. If they think that man creates to the extent he understands the God principle within him, they will never make a God from man, but they will make a man from God. Only the uninitiate will find contradiction in my statements. Those who have come to the real understanding of the great mystery of life will grasp the real meaning of the symbol we call language. They will also understand what we meant when we said that we are transformed into the qualities of our ideal by thinking it as a living and acting principle. The sum and substance of this metaphysics is, whatever qualities we attribute to our Ideal, the same mould our lives, if we let our Ideal have the full right of way in our daily lives. This is one of the greatest truths ever known to the metaphysical world. If you want to demonstrate any thing, first attribute all the necessary qualities to your Ideal, then try to feel that it is manifesting through you, and it is your constant companion. Whenever you will come to the point of perfect trust, calmness, and peace then you will know that your Ideal is coming into life or real significance to you. Our Ideal becomes real to the extent we put life into it by our thought or imagination. And we become the Ideal in the degree we let it manifest through us. Whatever we manifest the same we are. When we manifest the ability to sing, we become a singer. So in everything else. If our lives are the expression or manifestation of certain qualities we can manifest any quality we desire. It is our special privilege to do so, because all the qualities are our own creation and they exist only in this relative plane in our concept. As all of us have not the same concept so we have not the same sense of qualities. The music which charms a Chinese will not appeal to the sensitive ears of a white man, and vice versa. Yet through training one may learn to like a thing for which he has no liking. We begin to like a country and the people to the extent we change ourselves into their ideas. The only secret of changing ourselves into our ideal quality is to let it manifest through us. First have the clear picture of its attributes, then always feel that it is an acting and moving power in you, then submit yourself to the absolute guidance of it. When a man can have that trust and repose which adds courage to his conviction, he soon comes to live the life of his Ideal. This life is a great mystery, yet this mystery is so easily unveiled by the magic touch of knowledge.

IX

Some people are liable to ask, why should we submit ourselves to the guidance of our Ideal, when we know that it has no other qualities except what we attribute to it. Now the question is how these attributed qualities ever can have power to influence us. This query is natural for those who cannot think that an ideal can be anything else but an imaginary condition. But we ought not to forget the fact that our every thought reacts back on us, according to its nature. Suppose our ideal is nothing but our elevated concept, even then we cannot lose sight of its potency. Our higher concept reacts on us just as much as any thought or concept. Every thought or concept becomes a living force, according to the attributes we give it. In this relative plane we cannot conceive of any other life, except that which we become conscious of. Life there is in everything or everything is in one Life. Life alone is self-existant, and all other things exist because of that Life. If life alone is self-existant then all other things must be some forms of life, if they exist at all. However, we cannot recognize life in any thing, without being conscious of it. To be conscious of life in any thing we first attribute the qualities of life to it. That concept reacts on us and brings us to the realization of its life. You may call it imagination. Yes; it is imagination that rules the world, and also our relative lives. Without imagination there will be no creation. Everything we create or construct by the help of imagination. This imaging or imagining gives life to a shadow which reacts on our mind with the same force and vitality as any living being. When we are initiated into the mystery of this creation we find the life in every form and attribute. A piece of stone talks to a man when he gives attributes of life to it. Its message is so inspirational and devotional that it is simply marvelous. If it is all vague imagination of a distorted mind, then whence comes the sanely inspirational message which astounds the scientific mind. If we still maintain that it is the imagination regarding the attributes we give to a thing that affects our mind, then we have to admit that those attributes are living qualities. We have already stated that the thing without attributes or value has no significance to us. In other words a thing is no thing, without the value we attach to it. Then the very existence of a thing depends upon the recognition we give to it on account of its peculiar significance. Then our ideal must have a life and higher intelligence. There is but one life in this universe, therefore we and our ideals are one. The realization of the full life makes our life full. The Ideal is simply our life, which we already are, but which we have not yet realized. In the absolute plane everything is and nothing will be. But in the relative plane we come to realize the life which always is. This ever existant Life is in us and we are in this Life. Hence all these things and our ideals are all in us because we are in them.

53

Only by realization we know that it is all true. Those who have not the realization let them understand that our ideal is our better and greater life, and it can guide us safely through the rough road of the world. The man who knows that every thing is in God and there cannot be anything, even an idea or a thought beyond God, will find God in every thing. That does not mean that every thing is God. By giving a living attribute to a thing we impart life to it, but not by the exercise of our will power. We really make a thing living by giving a living attribute to it. In this world of life there cannot exist anything but the one life. So when we say we make a thing living by our living attribute we simply mean that we become conscious of that life which already exists. Our realization or non-realization makes a thing existant or non-existant. As far as the thing is concerned it may remain just the same. If a thing does not exist we cannot conceive its existence. If we conceive its existence it certainly exists. If we are convinced that it really does not exist in that particular form, then it surely exists in some other form. It is then, not the question of existence but of form. All that we see must have an existence, not in the forms as we see them but in essence. If the name of the forms is called matter, then it is a wrong name for that which eternally exists. But a wrong name cannot change the real nature and property of a thing. As far as we are concerned it may react on us according to our interpretation. It does not matter what name we give to a thing, but it matters what interpretation or meaning we give to that name. But we ought to bear this in our mind, that we cannot give any name to a thing if it does not exist at all. If we say that a piece of wood has no life, it does not prove that it has no life. If it does not come up to our definition of life, that simply means our definition of life is very limited. We define or give definition to a thing according to our concept. Since our concept changes, our definition cannot be a fixed idea. Our common sense will tell us that in this world of life there cannot be anything without life. If life is the only thing that exists then

54

a thing in itself must be a life. Therefore our definition of life is wrong. The thing which is self-existant needs no definition to qualify it. We always define a thing in the sense of comparison. The thing which is self-existant and eternal cannot have anything to compare with it. Therefore we cannot define it. Every thing has an eternal principle called life back of it. That means the thing which is nothing but name and form has the real essence back of it. That Something which is concealed by the wrong name and qualities is beyond all names. Therefore to call any thing into life is to go behind and beyond its form in our consciousness. As a visible man changes his expression with the coming of new life into him, so the visible thing when it pulsates with new life changes its expression. The new life in a thing means our new understanding of its existence. Our consciousness makes a thing new or old to us. It gives us new power and strength to combat with the circumstances which are our own creation. The difference between any two persons is their consciousness. Our struggle here is to attain to the higher and higher consciousness. It is that consciousness that the world is seeking. When we see a man is trying to master his situation we know that he is trying to be more conscious of his own power. Any effort to cope with conditions and things is an effort to come into more consciousness of power. The Supreme Consciousness is our goal. Little by little, step by step we are constantly moving towards that goal. When we realize that a consciousness is reached by the consciousness, we learn the secret of attaining power. We always reach our Ideal Consciousness by being conscious of its presence within us. When a consciousness communes with a consciousness higher than itself, it evolves into it. In this relative plane duality of concept is the natural logical consequence. Here in this plane we live the life of limited concept. In this plane we stand aloof from the rest of the creation. In this limited concept or consciousness we struggle to meet conditions, which are our own creation and which otherwise do not exist. Logically we know that all consciousness is within us, or that we are that consciousness. But we have not the realization. The problem we face here is how we can come into the realization of our Divine Oneness. As our life is a concept, so is our Divine Consciousness. By changing our smaller concept for the greater concept we become the greater concept. Some people call our ideal concept Subconscious Mind. Instead of Subconscious Mind if we call it the Cosmic Consciousness it will be more appropriate. Some people may raise an objection to the effect, that since our ideal concept is not perfect, it cannot be given the name Cosmic Consciousness. We ought not to forget that our concept of Cosmic Consciousness is also an imperfect concept, since we are imperfect. Our ideal concept is always perfect to us, or at least we give it the attribute of perfection. Though our ideal concept is our own creation on account of the attributes we give it, yet its power and potency is equal to its attributes, because every state or condition exists in the Absolute and it expresses the eternal life in proportion to our concept. If we do not doubt our existence, which is our concept, then there is no reason to doubt the existence of our Ideal. Then whatever attribute we give to our highest Ideal does not change its nature if it is ever existant. The attributes change us according to our better and greater concept of life, if we let them change us. Sub-conscious mind or God is our highest concept. According to the attributes we give it, it reacts upon us. There are no two minds as some people would have us believe. In fact, there is no mind in reality. Any thing which has attributes does not exist in the absolute sense. That does not change our position in this relative plane. What we think or believe, that exists. Our so-called Subconscious Mind is as conscious and intelligent as our conscious mind and infinitely more so. Whatever we anticipate our Subconscious Mind to do, the same it does. Our trust in the qualities we attribute to it, facilitates its reaction upon us. Some people, not understanding our meaning, are liable to think we do not believe in the higher power. We believe in the higher power just as

56

much as we believe in our own existence. It is the belief or thought that makes a thing thus and so. Master Jesus laid special stress on the belief. What a great mystery lies buried in the word belief.

X

The Subconsciousness or the great Cosmic Consciousness is dispassionate and non-attached. Its action is justified by our trust in the qualities we believe it to possess. Our relative existence ought not to be judged by the Absolute standard. Therefore let us accept that our life is a consciousness, so our Subconscious Mind is not a blind latent force in us. Since we are consciousness, we have reason to believe that we have come from a consciousness. By reaching up for the greater consciousness we gradually come to realize it. The concept, that on the background of one Great Consciousness we live, move, and have our being, is one of the grandest concepts in this world. When our Ideal inspires our action we act as divine beings. The human side of our nature is transmuted by divine concept. As long as we stand apart from the Great Cosmic Consciousness we feel the necessity for unity. Nothing establishes such a close relationship between us and our great Ideal as the thought that It is the moving and acting power in our lives. Yet some people are liable to maintain that it is nothing but thought or imagination. We should like to ask them, what is not thought or imagination. Sickness, death, happiness, misery all exist in our thought or imagination. If we partake of the nature of the thought we think, why will not the thought of the nearness of God affect our being? If you think or imagine a person to be your enemy, that thought will certainly make an enemy of that person. And that person will affect you with the quality of your own thought.

We are living in a marvelous world. Imagination or thought make us either angel or devil. That inner condition which is responsible for what comes to us is created by our thought. If a person suffers, it is because there is a condition within him, which is his own creation. Similarly if he enjoys, it is due to the same reason. Our physical concept of life and the belief in disease makes disease manifest through our physical body. When we see any part of the body is afflicted we at once seek the condition in the very soul or being of the person. If we can stir up one's very soul by an ideal concept, or bring about gradual change in him by changing his concept we can effect a cure, no matter what is his ailment. Sudden spiritual inspiration is able to cure more ailments than all the known methods. No cure is so permanent as the cure effected by the spiritual uplift, because it changes a person's entire nature and makes a new being of him. When a person becomes new, his old condition is cast off as it were. The simple trust in the higher power elevates our concept and makes us a new being. The more we think of the higher power, the more we receive that power. The quality of thought always affects us and our nature is transformed by it. If we want to be Godly we must think of God, and try to see Him in everything and every action. Nothing gives us such a sense of peace and security as the thought, that everything is the gift of the Almighty and every action is His will. Even in so-called misfortune, if we try to see the hand of God we can have peace and consolation. Not only that, we rise from the creation of man to that of God. We make a thing spiritual by giving it a spiritual concept. In this sense we change a thing in its significance. A changed thing has a changed effect on us. We ought to think that any gift of Spirit cannot be anything but spiritual. Hence all that we see is spiritual. When we use the word spirit we do not mean anything opposite to matter. We simply mean a condition beyond the range of limitation. It also indicates the higher power and wisdom. We ought not to forget that our thought makes a thing spiritual or material. As far as the thing itself is concerned it is always the same. In this sense all that we see is absolute. So long as we live in this relative consciousness we give relative attributes to the Absolute, making it appear relative. There is no other way for us to establish unity with the Absolute God. We must love our higher Ideal as a living personality. It is through love, one concept approaches the other. To love means to live the life of the object we love. The life of an object is its value, which gives it a certain significance. When we think of that value we become that value ourselves. This is why we call love unity. It fuses up two conditional existences into one. Then, again, through the quality of love we become loving. Therefore we ought to think of loving everything and all things. Once we come to the realization of the quality of love, it is easy for us to love our highest Ideal. Whenever we live the life of any person, we love him. Since we may not know how the real person is, we love him as we think him to be. This attraction for the person is due to the quality which we attribute to him and which is within us. Really we love the thing which is within us and not without. But in this relative plane a thing and its attribute mean the same thing to us. Because we cannot separate a thing from its attribute. Hence the attribute is the significance of a thing, or what makes a thing as we know it. Therefore when we love a thing we hold its picture, with all its attributes, within us. The picture which we hold in our mind seems to effect a change in us according to its quality or qualities. We have discovered that by holding the thought of God in us we become God-like in attributes. Some people are of the opinion that a mental picture of a thing or a condition changes us into its likeness. How far we become like our mental picture depends upon how far our attributed qualities correspond to it. We generally change into the likeness of the qualities of a thing, not into that thing. If we think of God and pray to Him without having a clear conception of His attributes we may not derive any benefit therefrom. A clear conception of an attribute transforms our nature into it. As a piece of iron put in the furnace takes the quality of the fire, so our mind conceiving the divine Ideal partakes of its attributes.

In these present days we often hear people speak of vibrations. Very few people have the right concept of it. What we call mental vibrations are nothing but our mental concepts or consciousness. Whatever we are conscious of, the same affects our mind according to its quality or qualities. These effects of qualities of things or thoughts are our vibrations. These vibrations we can transmit to others, as we use the term transmit, in the relative sense. When a person enters our room with discontentment or anger we feel his mental condition if we are sensitive. We can change our vibration into any quality by the quality of thought. They say every molecule of our body vibrates with our inner vibration or consciousness. Our body expresses the quality of a vibration. If our body is weak we can make it strong by setting up a vibration of strength. It is very hard for us to set up a vibration which opposes the one we already have in us. It generally creates a conflict in our mind, which is anything but conducive of the best result. The best method we know to change the vibration is to put our whole being in the divine furnace of power. That is to say, hold the thought that your body and mind belong to the Great Power. When we vibrate, we vibrate through our general concept. Therefore the result cannot be greater than our concept. Whenever any part of our body is afflicted we can make it right by giving that part of the body to the great Power of health. The moment we realize the Great Health is manifesting through us we are cured. Some people may pray to God to heal them. If they get well at all, it is because of their faith in the healing power of God. Here also we find the influence of the quality of concept. When a person realizes or knows that God, All-Health, is manifesting through him he gets well. By holding before him that Ideal he sets up a vibration within him which produces a corresponding vibration in his body, and specially in the afflicted part. The higher quality of thought produces the higher vibration. We ought not to forget that a diseased condition is also vibration from our concept. Those who have the vague abstract idea of God or the power of All-Health scarcely get any benefit by their affirmation or thought. If anyone wants to demonstrate this law, let him try to understand more of it, instead of affirming words without comprehending their meaning. When one understands or realizes this law, there will be no need of any affirmations.

XI

Some people try to hold the thought or affirmation that Almighty God is healing their ailments. This thought is good in its way. It may benefit some people if they have the realization of the God power. One defect of that affirmation is, that it may suggest a condition which is adverse to health, as when we say, "God is making me well," or "I'm getting well," at the same time admitting a condition to the contrary. Even our higher thought expresses through the quality of our concept. If we let the sunlight pass through a colored glass it takes the color of the medium through which it passes.

There are people, who, on account of their deep concentration or strong faith, can overcome the difficulty of adverse suggestion. Now we must find the system which works in all cases. We have stated many times, we state again, that we are to leave all our troubles and cares to our highest Ideal. We do not believe in affirming or denying a condition. We simply believe in always manifesting the Divine Power and in living in that consciousness. At first we ought to have a clear idea of the attributes we give to our Ideal, and then we ought to give ourselves or the afflicted part of our body to its care. Like quality of thought produces the like quality of vibration. When we raise the vibration of an afflicted part into the plane of our Ideal it is cured, because the quality of thought transforms it into its nature. We can demonstrate over our pains and aches in a short time, if we can form the right concept of this truth. By the silent thought or discourse within ourselves we gradually come to the proper understanding of the law. To the extent we feel or realize that our afflicted part or condition belongs to a higher power, we receive the benefit. When we are conscious of owning our body, its vibration corresponds to that of our inner condition and concept. But when we are conscious that it is owned by a higher power its vibration changes according to the quality of concept regarding our Ideal. Some people think too much of their physical body. They live in the physical, because they believe they exist only in the physical body, which they admit to be limited and perishable. It is not so much the thought of the body that makes them physical, but it is the quality of thought regarding it. This concept of quality creates a mental condition which corresponds to that of the physical. In fact, a mental condition is also physical. It is the concept which differentiates mind from the body. In reality there is no difference between the mind and the body. It is like a lighted lamp in a room at night. The greater the distance from the centre of light the less is the power of light. Yet it is the same light all through the room. So our body is also mind, only one stands further in our concept or consciousness than the other. Therefore a person thinking of his body too much, as separate from his mind, lowers his concept of life in such a degree that he partakes of all the qualities of that concept. That is why he is seen to suffer from all kinds of physical and mental ailments. The very thought of the body makes us conscious regarding things and conditions which belong to the concept. The best way to change our physical concept is to submit ourselves to a greater Power.

Those who trust in the greater power with the proper understanding never are in want of anything. They enjoy perfect health because peace abides with them. They draw unto them all that they need. To draw a thing to one's self simply means to arrive at the consciousness of possession. Everything exists within us. Because God is the only life and that life is the only thing. We being that life, are ourselves all things we see and desire. In the relative concept of life we may not realize it, but it does not change the position which the Absolute occupies. We know it is very hard for many to be conscious of possessing their desired objects. It is only a matter of realization. The only way we can come into the realization is to trust in our highest Ideal. This Ideal never fails us if we can have the perfect trust. This knowledge is the only knowledge worth having. Because when we have this knowledge we have everything we want. This knowledge in itself is the fulfillment of all desires. A man can afford to forget all the discourse put in this book, but he cannot afford to lose the knowledge which this book is trying to convey. Remember that if this life is a Reality then our highest Ideal, God, is a Reality. God will be of no significance to us in this relative plane, if we do not exist. The truth about this life is that we can make it what we want to. We can raise our concept of life to divine heights, or lower it to the very depths of ignorance. But it is the understanding which gives us power to move, act, and manifest whatever concept we desire to manifest. We can have whatever we want, if we know the law of our being. If we abhor suffering there is no need to suffer. We can avoid suffering only then, when we have the full knowledge of this law. It is not the condition which causes us to suffer, but our interpretation thereof.

Nothing influences our destiny so much as the imagination. What a wonderful hold it has upon our lives. We cannot consider ourselves without recognizing its most potent power. All of our creations, mental and physical, depend upon its universal potency. It seems as though every atom of this universe is revolving in its sphere and doing its bidding. This whole fanciful, unreal creation, is becoming real by its magic touch.

We are all proud of our higher sentiment and finer feeling. It will be impossible for us to conceive of them without the help of imagination. In fact, they are the creation of imagination. With the widening of our mental horizon we want to have a greater grasp of our greater Ideal. This Ideal is at first a fanciful creation of the imagination. Then gradually that fancy becomes a reality to us as we perceive new life and power in it. We naturally desire a condition which we imagine will give us greater happiness and comfort. Before we realize that condition we try to enjoy it in our imagination. This gives us the foretaste of happiness which inspires us to actualize that condition. There is an ever progressive element in the constitution of our being. One condition gives us the impetus to realize another. In this relative plane we are ever desirous of drawing comparison. Therefore any condition comparatively better than the other becomes our choice. It will be impossible for us to draw a picture of an unrealized condition without the imagination. Our religious sentiment, rational or irrational, always can be traced from our desire for better condition. This desire we partly satisfy in the fanciful creation of our imagination. An imagination is not always a vague nonproductive thought. When we give an imagination a certain quality or attribute it becomes the most productive power in the universe. Because by the thought of a certain quality in a thing or a person, we become that quality. Any thought or imagination inspiring higher and better condition will make us higher and better in our concept. If we are conscious of being better than yesterday, we are really better. No condition can be reality to us which lies beyond our consciousness or imagination. The condition which we realize and hope to realize is real to us. One condition is real because we have realized it and another condition is real because we have the foreglimpse of it in our imagination. Imagination not only gives us the realization of the thing and condition we hope for, but it also transforms our whole being into its quality. Its effect on the mind is great and its effect on the body is not less. Our body being the projection of our mind, imagination changes our body in ratio it changes the mind. To bring about a physical change it is necessary to set up a strong imagination which will change the mind or mental concept. Nothing changes or moulds our concept so easily as the imagination. We have seen people in intense physical suffering instantaneously healed by changing their mental concept through imagination. When you are able to see through the whole creation you will admit that there is no difference between body and mind. There are people who believe that no organic trouble can be healed by mind or Divine Power. How ridiculous this will seem to those who understand the law of being and who know that in the mental plane there is no such thing called organic or nervous afflictions. By changing the concept of life such diseases as cancer and paralysis have been healed. If there has been any failure in any case it is because that desire for the Great Ideal, which brings about complete change in being has not been aroused. Let anyone change his disposition and nature and he will change his whole being. A changed man naturally has a changed body and mind. A disease will hang on so long as you will nourish the old condition. After the recovery from a disease we notice some change in a man, though it may not be a complete change. If he falls back again to his old condition disease is liable to appear in some other form. Disease is nature's warning for a change for the better. Change a man not intellectually, but constitutionally, and you have cured his disease, no matter what it is. Let one constantly imagine that his higher Ideal is taking possession of him and guiding him higher and higher to the highest conception of life, which we call realization, and he will soon be a new man. He will be transformed into the quality of his thought or imagination. Therefore we hold before the people the highest concept of purity and morality. The very concept will make them purer and cleaner men. Some people, not understanding this law of being, think that if it is all imagination they can do what they please. Some of them give unbridled license to their sense desires. If they had but the faint glimpse of the fact, that a man is his concept or realization, they would have tried to realize a higher Ideal than mere sense gratification. Our sense desires are due to a concept, that they are the only things in this life. It is the lack of a higher Ideal and higher concept of life which makes a man sensuous. In reality there is no pleasure in sense gratification except the imaginary value we put to it. Then you will say that your higher sentiments are likewise imagination. Yes, they are imagination, but they give us greater pleasure and happiness, therefore they are of greater value to us. Change is the law of our relative life, because we live a relative concept of life. We are bound to draw comparison between two conditions. When we are convinced that we derive more pleasure from a thing we have not, we must have that thing or we will suffer. From experience we know that the moment we believe a thing to be better than the thing we already have, we are not satisfied any more with that thing. That is the law of our being. A man who keeps on progressing is always happy and contented. Imagination is a most important factor in our life. At the same time it is of no importance without its relative value. When we go over the religious history of the world we become doubtful regarding its beneficent work. Think of the most atrocious crimes perpetrated in the name of Jesus Christ in the past. Protestants and Catholics fought each other with a perfect sense of justice. Both imagined they were fighting for the right cause. If this was not imagination, then what? What a great influence imagination exerts in our life. If we keep on imagining a condition for any length of time with sincerity and faith that condition materializes to us, and we begin to think that condition is right. But when we do not find peace and happiness in a condition then we ought to know that that condition is not sustained by our better understanding or concept. That concept, which brings peace, contentment, love, sympathy, understanding, is the concept for us. Fanaticism is also a religion. It appeals to those who are emotional and superstitious. When a man soars high on the wings of imagination to realize an ideal condition promised to him, and is carried far away from the bound of reason he is apt to forget that his neighbor has the same right and liberty to follow whatever religious concept appeals to him most. However faulty his concept of the Ideal may be, he nevertheless manifests the qualities attributed to his Ideal. Being simple, sin-

66

cere, and honest, he has the implicit confidence and trust in the Almighty power of his Ideal. That is why he is sometimes seen to make wonderful demonstrations. Demonstrations are demonstrations, they are neither due to good nor evil power. It is the man's concept that reflects back on him and makes a power good or evil. Then a person may not have the same high concept of his Ideal as we have, in a comparative sense, yet judging from his power of understanding we cannot help but admit that his concept of Ideal is as perfect to him as ours to us. The cosmic concept of God which establishes the brotherhood of man and the fatherhood of God is the highest and best concept the human mind can conceive of. The next best concept is God dwelling within us as a motive power in our life. Then comes the concept of God in nature. This concept is the beginning of the cosmic concept of God. Here we find the nature manifesting the life and intelligence, and reacting upon our consciousness with the presence of God. From this state we notice the possibility of our reaching that sublime height of spiritual unfoldment we call Cosmic Consciousness. The other phases of idealism below these are limited by human passions and desires. Therefore their worshipers manifest through them the qualities attributed to their Ideal in exaggerated forms. In all these we learn this lesson, that the human nature is always rushing forward to meet the Divine Nature. Therefore we fully agree with the statement that religion is the primordial instinct in man. Toleration and brotherly love are the basic concept in the teaching of the Master Jesus. When we establish unity through love with all that manifests God life we live, move, and have our being in the vitalizing current of Cosmic Life. God is our Soul of souls. He is so near, yet so far away in our concept that unity sometimes seems to be far off. But if we follow the footsteps of the Master Jesus it is easy for us to establish unity with God. By the constant thought of His presence in us we come to feel His Presence. Therefore nothing is like the thought, that the Almighty God is manifesting through us and guiding us to the higher and higher sphere of life or consciousness. The higher concept of God makes a man Godly. God is love, and love means unity or Yoga. Our supreme goal is "I and my Father are one."

The Light of Christian Yoga

Question.—What is the meaning of Yoga?

Answer—The literal meaning of Yoga is to join, bind or to unite. The special meaning of Yoga is a means by which we unite ourselves with God, the great universal Principle.

Question.—What do we mean by the word life in the special sense of the term?

Answer.—We mean that indestructible principle which never changes, and which is beyond time, space, and condition.

Question.—What is human life then?

Answer.—It is a limited concept of our being which is subject to change. We ought to remember that a concept can never change that which is unchangeable. A concept is a mere opinion or idea regarding our life and the things which seem attached to it, but it is not the real life.

Question.—Can there be anything beyond Life?

Answer.—No; there cannot be, since Life is omnipresent, and the only principle or thing that ever exists. If Life is all-in-all and absolute there cannot exist anything beyond it.

Axiom.—No two things can occupy the same space. In this relative plane, according to this axiom, Omnipresent Life and another thing cannot occupy the same space.

Question.—Can we give any attribute to Life, which is beyond time, space and condition?

Answer.—No; we cannot give it any attribute. Whenever we give any attribute to any thing we limit it. Our concept of ourselves being limited, we cannot give any attribute to any thing which will not be limited. Then again all attributes or qualities are relative. Without the relative concept of a thing, we cannot think of its qualities. For example, when we say that a flower is red, we convey the idea that it is of no other color but that which we call red. We cannot give any attribute to that which

69

is the only existant and has nothing to compare with it. Therefore it is beyond all relative conditions and attributes.

Question.—Do we not give attribute to Life when we say it is Omnipresent?

Answer.—Yes; we do. We cannot use the word Omnipresence without referring to the space. That which is beyond space cannot be of space. Space exists only in our concept. We recognize space from our sense of distance. That which is all-in-all does not require to go or move anywhere. Therefore, It is beyond space. Without referring to space we can only say, It simply exists. But to express it through the human concept of space, we must say It is Omnipresent. If Life is all-in-all then our concept of space must be in that Life. Then again our concept of space being in that Life, that Life must be in our concept. Take for example, a ring immersed in the sea. As the sea exists in the band of the ring, without being limited, so the Absolute Life exists in our limited concept without being limited. Hence whatever concept of God we may have, we find Him in that concept.

Question.—What is sin?

Answer.—It generally means a condition detached or divorced from the light or truth. It also means limitation or limited concept. Whenever we limit ourselves by not giving response to the demand of our higher Self or better understanding we sin against the law of our being.

Question.—What do we mean by death of sinful life?

Answer.—We simply mean an end to the limited concept, through many unpleasant experiences or sufferings. Our concept is our life. Whatever concept it may be, it is ever subject to change. In this sense, all lives of limited concept must come to an end. Because they are all sinful, mortal lives.

Question.—What do we mean by mortality?

Answer.—We mean a relative condition which is subject to change.

Question.—Are we immortal or mortal?

Answer.—In the relative sense we make ourselves mortal or

immortal by our thought. In the absolute sense we are always immortal, because we are that which is self-existent and without change.

Question.—How can we come to the realization of our immortality?

Answer.—By forming a relative concept of that which is immortal. We partake of the quality of a thought and become that quality ourselves. The thought, that we are immortal in essence, brings us the realization of immortality.

Question.—What should we do when we find it hard to hold the thought of immortality, on account of the opposing suggestion?

Answer.—We hold the thought that the immortal essence is manifesting through our life and constantly guiding us to the goal of realization.

Question.—How can we come to the realization of our Divine Oneness?

Answer.—By meditating upon the idea that we are coming to the realization. If it is too abstract and vague, then let us think that the Divinity is manifesting through us and bringing us the realization.

Question.—If one tries to understand the truth and is anxious to get realization, but does not get the desired result, what is he to do?

Answer.—We ought not to try to understand the truth on our own responsibility. We ought to surrender ourselves to the absolute guidance of the Divine Power. Whoever will trust in that power and take no thought of himself and his desires will receive in time whatever he desires. It is a fixed law which never changes or fails.

Question.—What do we mean by the word demand, and how are we to demand any thing of the great universal law of supply?

Answer.—The real significance of the word demand is mere wish or desire. Whenever we demand any thing of the law we should simply make our desire known and leave everything to its absolute guidance. When we understand the law, nothing can be simpler than this. It works miracles.

Question.—How can we understand this law?

Answer.—By meditation or dwelling upon the operation of the law. The quickest way to come to the understanding of law is to leave the matter under the guidance of the Ideal. The understanding, or the realization, comes to those who can live in the consciousness that the hand of the Almighty is guiding them. Almighty God being within us, by directing our consciousness we become conscious of His presence.

Question.—What is meant by an error thought?

Answer.—It is a thought that is inharmonious with the great principle of Life.

Question.—How can we help not holding the error thought, as long as we live in this relative concept of life?

Answer.—Our principal aim is to rise above this changeable concept by realizing more of that which is unchangeable. By thinking more of that unchangeable principle, we partake of the quality of that thought, and thereby rise above the error-thought.

Question.—Is there any thought called right or wrong?

Answer.—In reality there is no thought called right or wrong. But in this relative plane our thought becomes right or wrong according to our concept. We judge a thought from the standpoint of our better understanding. Therefore each of us determines a thought right or wrong according to the light in which he understands it. In this relative plane we change our opinion of right or wrong according to the change of our understanding.

Question.—What is meant by a concept?

Answer.—A concept is our opinion or idea regarding ourselves and the things pertaining to us. We may also call it our understanding or consciousness.

Question.—How can we change our concept?

Answer.—By holding the thought for the better understanding and believing that some higher power is leading us to the better concept of life.

Question.—Why are we moulded by the nature of our thought?

Answer.—The nature of thought means its quality. By dwelling upon a thought of certain quality we become that quality. Thus we are moulded or become the nature of our thought. The reason we become the nature of our thought, is because of the law, that we partake of the quality of thoughts we think. Our concept is our thought-creation, and it is our life. The life which is created by the nature of thought is also moulded by the nature of thought.

Question.—How can we secure calmness and peace within ourselves?

Answer.—By trusting in our great Ideal, God. When we hold the thought, that He is taking care of us and our wants, we have nothing to worry us. When we do not worry we have calmness and peace within us.

Question.—What is meant by entering the kingdom of God?

Answer.—It means entering into a condition of calmness, peace and trust.

Question.—How do we live, move, and have our being in God?

Answer.—We are already in God. In this world of God nothing can exist but Him. We, by the realization of His presence, come to live, move, and have our being in Him. It is simply a matter of consciousness.

Question.—What is an Ideal?

Answer.—Christian Yoga uses that term in the place of God. God being a vague, indefinite term and of mythological origin, we use the word Ideal, denoting our highest concept of power and intelligence, and which is not arbitrary in deciding our destiny.

Question.—What makes us doubtful of attaining our Ideal?

Answer.—It is lack of proper understanding of our relation with our Ideal which makes us doubtful of attaining it.

Question.—How can we conquer fear and doubt?

Answer.—Fear and doubt spring from ignorance and limitation. We can conquer them by holding the thought that a higher

73

power is always protecting us. The more direct way to allay them is to manifest the greater power and intelligence.

Question.—How can we overcome self-consciousness?

Answer.—By thinking less of ourselves. When we bear our own burden we cannot help but think of ourselves. But if we can shift all our cares and burdens to our Ideal, by manifesting the same, we will have no occasion to think of ourselves.

Question.—Can we conceive of any thing without the suggestion of its opposite, such as good and bad, light and darkness?

Answer.—No; not in this relative plane.

Question.—How can we change the significance of polar opposites?

Answer.—By using them in the comparative sense, not in the opposite. For example, instead of taking darkness as opposed to light, we ought to take it in the sense of less light.

Question.—How can we overcome the suggestion of a polar opposite?

Answer.—By not thinking of it, and by manifesting our Ideal through us.

Question.—What is disease?

Answer.—It is lack of harmony with our legitimate concept or understanding.

Question.—Where lies the seat of a disease?

Answer.—It is deep down in our being or in our concept.

Question.—How can we cure a disease?

Answer.—By changing our concept for the better.

Question.—How can we change our concept for the better?

Answer.—By holding the better quality of thought.

Question.—In case of sickness, is the thought of health the better quality of thought?

Answer.—Yes, it is, provided it does not make us more conscious of our sickness.

Question.—What is the best way to regain health in sickness?

Answer.—Not to deny or affirm sickness, but to let the All-Health our Ideal, manifest through us. We manifest our Ideal by holding the thought that It is manifesting through us, and

74

it has taken possession of our whole being. We are under Its absolute guidance.

Question.—In what respect is this method superior to anything else, and what special advantage do we gain?

Answer.—It does not hold any suggestion of polar opposites, anl it brings about a change in us by changing our concept. We gain our health quicker than by any thing else, by the quality of a higher thought.

Question.—What is the new discovery of the Christian Yoga healing?

Answer.—The quality of a thought works both physical and mental change in our being. When a person thinks of his own body, it takes the condition which already exists in him. But when he thinks that his body belongs to a higher power, it takes the condition or quality of that Ideal. As a piece of iron in a blazing furnace partakes of the quality of the fire, so our body and mind submitted to the highest Ideal partakes of Its quality. If a person can constantly hold the thought that his afflicted part belongs to his Ideal he is sure to get well.

Question.—Can all people hold the thought of their Ideal when they suffer from sickness?

Answer.—Yes; they can if they try, though it may be hard in serious illness.

Question.—What is the best way to reach those who are suffering intensely and cannot hold any thought of an Ideal?

Answer.—They must surrender themselves to the care of some one who understands the law and manifests his Higher Ideal.

Question.—Are all diseases curable?

Answer.—Yes; they are.

Question.—What about the organic diseases?

Answer.—There is no such thing as organic disease. Our whole physical and mental system is one, no matter by what name we call it. This system is sustained by our concept. When we are able to change our concept by the higher quality of thought, we become free from disease of all forms.

Question.—Why are some healers more successful in their practice than others?

Answer.—The success of a healer depends upon his faith in his power and his patient's faith in him. What he believes and knows that he radiates.

Question.—What kind of people make the most successful healers?

Answer.—Those who are plain and simple, and have the grasp of the law more by intuition than by reason. That is why the plain and simple disciples of the Master Jesus became the best healers in the world.

Question.—Why does the realization or understanding of the law surpass all scientific methods of healing?

Answer.—By realizing the law we are able to determine the cause and cure of a disease.

Question.—Can anyone cure a disease without changing his patient's concept?

Answer.—If the cure is radical it is impossible to cure any one without changing his concept in which lies the seat of a disease.

Question.—How many forms of disease do we recognize?

Answer.—Only one. They are all due to one condition. If that condition is not changed the radical cure will be impossible. When we cure one form of disease in a person and fail in another form, we know that the cure is not complete. We simply change the form but not the cause of disease.

Question.—What is the difference between Christian Yoga and other new methods of healing?

Answer.—Christian Yoga advocates the surrendering of oneself to one's Ideal or highest concept of Power and to manifest that Ideal through the being, while other new forms of healing believe in affirming for health or the denial of disease.

Question.—Why are affirmations not always effective?

Answer.—All affirmations suggest polar opposites. Their effectiveness is determined by the mental condition of the one who affirms. If a person has strong faith in an affirmation or strong concentration, so that an opposite suggestion cannot detract his mind, he derives some benefit from an affirmation. We affirm for a condition opposite to that which we want to overcome or eliminate. If that affirmation suggests this very condition we want to overcome it will be ineffective.

Question.—What can best take the place of affirmations?

Answer.—The Christian Yoga method, that is to manifest our perfect Ideal.

Question.—What is meant by a positive demand?

Answer.—It is a demand with positive knowledge. When we understand the proper meaning of a demand and are sure of its fulfillment that demand is positive.

Question.—What is the difference between thought and feeling?

Answer.—A thought is a mental action, while feeling is the realization of a thought or a condition.

Question.—Why should we not resist evil?

Answer.—Because by resisting evil we become conscious of its Power. The more conscious we become of a condition the more influence it exerts on us. Every time we try to resist it, it becomes stronger in power. In time we are overcome by the evil, on account of the quality of thought.

Question.—How should we overcome evil?

Answer.—In the first place it is better not to admit evil as opposed to good. In the second place it is better not to try to overcome it at all. Only by hinking of good we overcome evil, by partaking of and radiating the quality of that thought. Every time we think evil we become evil. We ought not to forget that good overcometh evil, not by the thought of overcoming, but by its quality.

Question.—What is dislike and hate?

Answer.—It is an inharmonious or discordant feeling within oneself. The metaphysical meaning of hate is, taking away a quality or qualities from a thing or person, which is equal to deducting those qualities from oneself.

Question.—What is love?

Answer.—Love is unity.

Question.—What is meant by salvation?

Answer.—Salvation means freedom from the relative concept.

Question.—What is relative concept?

Answer.—Concept of relative values regarding things and conditions. Such as one thing being better than the other, good and bad.

Question.—What is meant by sub-conscious?

Answer.—The literal meaning of the word is faintly conscious, applying to perceptions which are without consciousness or memory. Some writers apply that word to a mind, which is supposed to be dormant and can be developed by suggestive means. Metaphysically, there cannot be a mind without consciousness or memory, but there can be a state. That state is relative to us. We become conscious to a degree we realize our universal consciousness. It is rather coming to the consciousness than developing consciousness.

Question.—What is faith?

Answer.—The literal meaning of faith is the capacity of the soul whereby spiritual truth is apprehended, and spiritual life engendered. Faith really means the comprehension of truth by intuition and the trust therein. It is knowledge.

Question.—What is wisdom?

Answer.—Wisdom means knowledge, specially self-knowledge.

Question.—Can we not hold an Ideal condition of ourselves instead of an Ideal which is distinct from us?

Answer.—Yes, we can. But the result may not be as satisfactory. In this relative plane we are more or less self-conscious. The Ideal condition which we hope for is not a realized condition. While we may be trying to reach or realize it our old condition may re-assert itself. Because we are liable to be conscious of two conditions, the one we want to overcome and the other we want to realize. It is very hard for many to control two relative conditions without being conscious of both. The condition which we have within us will have greater influence over us if we are conscious of it, than the one we hope to realize. But when we let our Ideal work through us as a living consciousness and we

78

are conscious of its action we have very little occasion to think of our old condition. At least we have no cause to invite it to our consciousness. When we have very little or nothing to do with a condition, good or bad, it cannot force itself into our consciousness. At the same time by the constant thought of our Ideal we partake of its qualities and soon we are transformed into them. This is one of the principal points of Christian Yoga.

Question.—What is the difference between the old orthodox idea of God and the Christian Yoga Ideal?

Answer.—The orthodox God is a fixed entity with the arbitrary power to punish and reward a person and who is far away from the human being. The Christian Yoga Ideal is a part of our being. The relation between us and our Ideal is so close that nothing can separate us. Then by the holding of this Ideal there is nothing to fear or to lose, but everything to gain. We may neglect and drive away our Ideal. It is never offended. When we invite It again It comes back to us with the same degree of love and cordiality as we extend to It. It is simply grand and sublime. It always acts through the reflection of our own soul. That permanent, dispassionate, immanent Ideal takes the part of any concept we may have of It. Only those who have the realization will understand it. Those that are without, to use the Master's expression, will think we create a God only to satisfy our whim.

Question.—Is there any other God aside from the one we create?

Answer.—We create no God, we simply create a concept of Him. In this relative plane we see everything according to our concept. Above our concept, if a thing exists at all, it must be the Absolute. So we do not create anything in the sense of creator since there is nothing to create, everything is, but we create a concept regarding something that exists permanently. This concept gives us the idea of form. In this universe only one thing exists and that thing is beyond all change and form. These forms as we see them around us are not the real forms of that which eternally exists, but these forms are the creation of our concept. Therefore, when we come to the realization of the Supreme One, all these forms vanish from our sight. We see nothing but God. Some people, through mistake, call this visible universe also God. This visible universe exists only in our concept, in reality it does not exist. Our concept regarding a thing and the thing itself is not one and the same. Yet without something real we cannot form a concept. Consequently a concept, right or wrong, always refers to some thing which is reality and Truth. Whatever may be our concept of God and the universe, it always means the same thing, that is, it is a concept of something which is real and permanent.

Question.—What is the best way to worship God?

Answer.—Anyway we may think best for us. No matter in what form or concept we worship God with the proper understanding and in spirit, we reach the goal of realization.

Question.—In what spirit should we worship God?

Answer.—We are not to worship a form or concept but the great principle which it represents.

Question.—Is it possible to worship God without a form or a concept?

Answer.—Not as long as we exist in this relative plane and concept. Form does not necessarily always mean a visible form, it also means an idea. The word form or concept means the same thing. Because all visible and invisible forms are nothing but our ideas or concepts.

Question.—How can we come to the realization of the absolute God?

Answer.—By giving Him higher and higher attributes and meditating upon them.

Question.—Why does the idea of unity with the absolute God unsettle the mind of many people, and cause them to feel a sense of loss and discomfort?

Answer.—Because they are attached to their material conditions or concepts.

Question.—What is the best way to unfold their consciousness?

Answer.—First to form a definite concept of their Ideal and next to let that Ideal have full sway in their lives.

Question.—What are they to do if they have desires for the material things and pleasures which we know to be unreal?

Answer.—Our desires are never satisfied if we keep on feeding them. However, our desires for the material things come from our concept. Only by changing the concept, one can rise above all material desires. If anyone wants his desires fulfilled he must learn to leave everything in the hands of his Ideal. Whenever we receive anything as a gift of our Ideal we enjoy it on account of the higher quality of that thought.

Question.—How can we love our Ideal which is not tangible?

Answer.—We always love the attributed quality or qualities of a thing or a person. Without imagining those qualities in our object of love we cannot love it. It matters very little whether it possesses those qualities or not, though we make ourselves believe that it possesses them. Sometimes our attributed qualities may correspond to that which the object is manifesting through its concept. However, whenever we attribute any quality to a thing or a person we simply attribute that which is within us. In fact we love that which is within us, but not any object or person outside of us. Therefore we can love the Ideal which is within us and manifesting through us by attributing our desired qualities.

Question.—What do we mean when we say, our concept needs more life?

Answer.—It means our concept needs expansion, that is, a wider concept of life. To be conscious of more life is to express more life.

Question.—Can the qualities attributed to an imaginary object appear in an objective form?

Answer.—Yes, they can, though that form may be invisible to others. By stronger concentration we can manifest it to others, provided there is no counteracting thought in operation. But the less we discuss such a subject the better it is for us. By discussing it and trying to produce phenomena of that sort we distract our attention from the real goal of life. We ought to remember that we always take the quality of the thought we think.

Question.—How can we materialize our desires without concentrating upon our desired objects?

Answer.—In this objective plane every action has reaction, whenever we desire any thing, according to the quality of thought it reacts upon us. Concentration and the quality or nature of a desire for an object, are not the same. A quality of a desire changes us, because we become that quality ourselves by holding it in our minds. We naturally find response from objects which correspond to our being or concept. Our desires are materialized to the extent our concept corresponds to the desired object. In other words whenever we deserve anything it comes to us whether we solicit it or not. Hence materialization of our desires means changing our concepts into the attributed qualities of the object we desire. If our mind is not disturbed or ruffled our nature is transformed quickly into the quality of a thought or of a desire. A mere wish on our part for a thing is enough to bring response from the great Law of supply. When we understand the law we never desire anything which is not best for our spiritual unfoldment. Peace and calmness we must have first, before we attempt to demonstrate the law. By surrendering ourselves to the absolute guidance of our Ideal we can easily secure calmness and peace.

Question.—What is the value of concentration then?

Answer.—Concentration stops the distraction of our mind, that is, it holds our minds to one point. It is conducive to the best results in our work.

Question.—How can we develop our concentration?

Answer.—By thinking less of it and being more interested in the subject at hand.

Question.—How can we get interested in a subject which we do not like?

Answer.—By cultivating a liking for it and imagining it is not tedious.

Question.—How can we develop a liking for a subject?

Answer.—By thinking that it is not we but our Ideal that is liking it. It is easy to solve all our difficulties, trials and tribulations through our Ideal.

Question.—How can we gain understanding and peace when overwhelmed with the problems and mysteries of this life?

Answer.—By letting our Ideal guide us. In the fullness of time, that is, when we are ready to grasp, our Ideal will reveal to us whatever is necessary for our unfoldment.

Question.—Can suffering bring spiritual unfoldment?

Answer.—There is no such condition called suffering in reality.—By admitting the condition of suffering in our concept we have suffering. That is why we suffer from it. The condition which we call suffering is inevitable in this relative plane if we believe in it. It simply indicates an effort on the part of our being to come out of the old condition. A person who is ever progressive or ever giving response to his better understanding knows no suffering. Therefore suffering is a wise provision of the law of our being to lead us on and on to the better life and understanding. Yes, it helps our spiritual unfoldment to the extent we understand its purpose. When we see a new light through suffering we become free from it.

Question.—Does a spiritually minded man suffer from physical ailments?

Answer.—Yes, he does if he believes in the physical ailments. We do not partake of any quality which we do not attribute to our Ideal.

Question.—Can we cure all cases of disease by the Christian Yoga method of healing?

Answer.—Yes, we can if the patients understand the fundamental principle of the Yoga method. It is so simple yet it is so hard for many to have the full grasp of it. If they can grasp this one Idea that we partake of the quality of a thought, they can be cured.

Question.—What is the best way to convey to others the idea of quality of thought?

Answer.—By drawing the illustration of a piece of iron in the fire. As the piece of iron partakes of the quality of the fire, so when we give our afflicted part to our highest Ideal, it partakes of Its Quality.

Question.—What is the cause of our committing so-called sin?

Answer.—Because of our ignorance and attachment to the old condition. Progress is the law of our being. Whenever we fail to give response to the demand of our nature or being we commit sin.

Question.—Is this visible world real?

Answer.—No; it is not in the absolute sense. But in the relative sense everything, which we think to be real is real. Even in this unreal world there is a real substance which is eternal and immortal.

Question.—Is there any value in a thing except the value which we give to it?

Answer.—No; the value of a thing exists only in our concept. This value changes with the change of our concept. That goes to prove that there is no permanent value in a thing.

Question.—Is happiness reality or imagination?

Answer.—In this relative plane happiness and misery are both our concept, due to imagination.

Question.—If it is all imagination why do we think happiness and misery to be real?

Answer.—They are real if we think them to be so. We cannot go beyond our own understanding and feeling, unless we rise above it by expanding our concept.

Question.—Why do we form an attachment for a being, thing or condition?

Answer.—Because we think it is real and a source of happiness.

Question.—How can we learn to see God in all things?

Answer.—In the absolute sense nothing exists but God. In

84

the relative sense all these things which we see exist in our concept. To see God in all things really means to see Him in our concept. When we see God in our concept, our concept becomes Godly. In other words, our concept manifests Godly qualities. That which we manifest, the same we attribute to the things we see around us. Now the question is, how can we see God in our concept, or how can we enlarge our concept? First we take the help of our imagination. With the help of our imagination we try to see the living expression of God in everything. This imagination at times becomes a reality. Then we wake up to find the whole universe pulsating with God-life. On looking within we find the same Life is manifesting through us. That is to say, when all things come to exist in the ocean of divine consciousness we ourselves come to exist in the same. All the outside conditions are but the reflection of our inner concept or realization.

Question.—How can a thing come to Life?

Answer.—Life there is everywhere. In fact we see that life in the form of a thing on account of our concept. However, to see life in a thing, is to come to the realization of it, through our concept, that is why we see the life and the thing as spearate from each other although they are one. A thing does not come to life, since it is the life misnamed and misconceived, but we come to realize that life through our relative concept.

Question.—Shall we accept this life as an illusion?

Answer.—An intellectual understanding does not necessarily correspond to our realization. We cannot live the life more than we have realized. We may live a life in the anticipation of greater realization, but that is not our life, since our life is what we have realized. If we have really come to the realization that this life is an illusion, then there will be no need of asking that question. Because we ask a question in order to form a correct idea or opinion regarding a thing, condition or a person. A question indicates a condition of doubt or ignorance, which cannot be a positive knowledge or realization. Hence we ought to begin our life according to our concept of better understanding, which does not stand far away from our realization. But we ought to always keep the highest Ideal before us.

Question.—Then what is the use of metaphysical discourse?

Answer.—The intellectual discourse of such a subject stands before us as a beacon light in the distant horizon. It always inspires us to march on and on until we have reached the goal of realization. Then by reading and studying such a subject we come to the realization quicker, by the quality of thought.

Question.—How often should a person read this metaphysics?

Answer.—The oftener the better. The more we read the more light we receive.

Question.—Should we read any other treatise while reading this metaphysics?

Answer.—There is no restriction. It is better for us to have the full comprehension of this "Life and the Way" first before we take up another book of a similar subject. By centralizing our force and doing one thing at a time we gain the best results. We ought not to forget the fact, that by reading metaphysics we are only able to see a light in our mental vision, but by silent work we come to the realization.

Question.—What is matter?

Answer.—It depends upon what our concept is regarding it, in this relative plane. If, by the word matter we mean something opposite to spirit then it does not exist, because it cannot exist. Nothing opposite to the Absolute can exist. It is all in all. If by matter we mean that which is visible and tangible, then it cannot be a reality, since all things visible exist only in our concept. If it is the projection or differentiation of spirit, then it cannot exist in the absolute sense, since the absolute is beyond all change and form. If by matter we mean the miscalled spirit, then it is nothing but a name of the Spirit. A name may designate an object, but it cannot qualify it. Even the adjective which qualifies a noun cannot change the constitutional nature of it. Hence if matter is a miscalled name for the Self-existent Spirit it cannot have any relation to it. What is matter then? Can we deny it? No; for the very reason we have admitted

86

its existence by giving it a name we cannot deny it. The thing which does not exist does not require to be denied or affirmed. Consequently matter exists but it exists only in name. When we try to solve the problem from our relative understanding or plane we find another side of the question. Since our life is real because our concept or thought makes it so, everything pertaining to this life is also real. Then matter which is tangible to our sense perception is a reality. If everything is real in this universe, then matter is self-existent and unchangeable. Then matter and spirit are one. But since matter in our concept changes, it cannot be unchangeable spirit. Then we cannot say that this changeable matter is real. Some people maintain, that matter is the quality of spirit, in the same sense as the sun rays of the sun. Like the sun and its rays spirit and matter are inseparable. The Absolute cannot have a quality, since it is all in all and there is nothing to qualify it. A quality really belongs to the relative plane where we can compare two or more numbers of things. Hence matter cannot be the quality of spirit. It is really spirit in name, that is, the spirit is so-called and so seen on account of our concept.

Question.—Is there any life inherent in matter?

Answer.—No; there cannot be. There cannot be any life in a name, but the thing it stands for is the life itself. If we see any life in matter at all, it is because of our concept. When we see life in anything we see life in our concept.

Question.—What is the difference between spirit and matter?

Answer.—Just as much difference as between a person and his name. As a person does not change by any name we call him, so spirit does not change by the attribute we may give it.

Question.—What is meant by physical death?

Answer.—There is no such word as death in the dictionary of metaphysics. Death is a belief in the departure of life from the physical body. According to the limited concept of the world it also means disintegration or destruction. We know this so-called physical manifestation is nothing but our concept, which is just as unreal as matter. But in the relative concept this body is a reality. Like all other so-called real things it is subject to change according to our concept. If we have the realization of our real Self, we rise above the concept of change. Then we can assume and retain any form we want to. Until then this body will undergo the change, which we call death.

Question.—Will the person who has the realization ever desire to take any form?

Answer.—No; then he is above all desire, he is awake from his dream.

Question.—Can any one retain this physical form as long as he wants to?

Answer.—Yes; he can if he understands the law. To retain the physical form does not mean to retain the same quality of concept. It means to give constant response to the demand or requirement of our higher concepts. The demand of our being is the spiritual unfoldment, that is, the change of our lower concept into higher. When we cease to give response to that demand, our physical body, which is the manifestation of our old concept, becomes old.

Question.—How can we be happy with misery apparent all around us?

Answer.—By thinking less of the misery. Yes, it is hard to do it when we have the misery all around us, because of the constant suggestion. By depending on our Ideal to adjust conditions and living the life of trust and peace, we can be happy under any circumstances.

Question.—Can anyone be healed regardless of his belief?

Answer.—Yes; if he will conform to a simple requirement he will be healed. If he can trust himself entirely to the care of a healer and follow his simple directions, he can be healed regardless of his belief.

Question.—What is spirit?

Answer.—There is no such thing called spirit as opposite to matter. If the term refers to the Absolute then the word means that which is everlasting and eternal, above all qualifications. The word Spirit was originally used in the sense of invisible energy.

Then it was understood to be the substance out of which all things were created. The next best concept of it was that which dwelled in everything and which was indestructible. When the transitory nature of things was considered it was found that things, which had a beginning, must have an end. Then it became evident that the spirit which seemed to depart or die with the dissolution of matter must be mortal. With the greater realization humanity came to know, that spirit was that which was self-existent and which was never born and never died.

Question.—What is immortal?

Answer.—That which is never born and never dies. The thing which has a beginning must have an end. Then, if for the sake of argument we say that the essence of things is unchangeable, though their forms may be destroyed, then we have to admit, that their forms which give us impressions of reality of things are not immortal. According to our definition of immortality this world of form cannot be real or immortal. Hence the immortal has no form.

Question.—Can God be known as He really is?

Answer.—Yes; when we know ourself we know God. But when we know God as He is we no more exist in this relative plane. Then in consciousness we become as one with God. When we say we know God we mean the realization of God. What we realize, that we are.

Question.—How shall we convey this truth to others?

Answer.—By taking no thought, whether it be accepted or rejected. At the same time we must gain power and strength in our silent meditation. We cannot give this truth to others, if we have not made it our own by the realization. We ought to remember that when all external means fail, our inner power and realization stands good for us.

Question.—Does our external effort succeed, if we have not the inner power to back us up?

Answer.—No; no matter what we undertake to do we can never successfully carry it out, if we have not the realization of the power within us.

Question.—How should we know the right time for action?

Answer.—If we sit calmly and quietly for our Ideal to direct us, we will find no difficulty to ascertain it.

Question.—Can anyone succeed in life without knowing the law?

Answer.—Yes; he can, but in order to succeed he must unconsciously follow this law. Success is much easier to attain, if one consciously knows and follows the law.

Question.—What advantage have we if we follow this law?

Answer.—We never worry, fret or spend our time in anxiety and restless anticipation. The right mental condition brings success to us. The proper mental attitude is expressed in the following: "The Lord is my Shepherd, I shall not want."

Question.—What should we do when opposition and adversity confronts us?

Answer.—Hold the thought that the Lord is my life and guide and I can not have any opposition. The great secret of this life is, that our faith in our higher power overcomes all difficulties and opposition. In this relative plane our concept is our being, and in this domain of concept, higher concept rules the lower. Once we understand this law, nothing is so grand and beautiful.

Question.—How should we act in danger and difficulty?

Answer.—First, to trust in the guidance of our Ideal and then, to follow our inner prompting. We should not plan ahead of time by our limited knowledge.

Question.—Can anyone borrow this truth and preach it as his own?

Answer.—No; no one can borrow this truth. It is a common wealth and it is for those who seek it. Without understanding this truth no one can accept it. It belongs to whomsoever understands it, and our blessing should go with him.

Question.—How may we inspire others to do their best?

Answer.—By setting an example before them.

Question.—What should we do when envy and jealousy overpower us?

Answer.—We should sit quietly and hold the thought, that this life belongs to the great Ideal; we have nothing to be jealous of; and the same Ideal is working through others; we are all one in that Spirit.

Question.—What is the best thought to entertain on retiring?

Answer.—That to-day I have received what I have earned, and I am thankful to my great Ideal for manifesting this wisdom through me. That nothing comes to me if I do not earn it. Whatever I receive is for my greater and higher realization. My life and guide is my Ideal and It is always with me. *Om peace.*

Question.—Why did Christ tell us to love our enemies?

Answer.—We cannot have any other enemy than the one we recognize. Our feeling towards our enemies is anything but kind and loving. When we love them they cannot remain our enemies any more. Love is unity and God. By loving our enemies we not only become free from the inharmonious thought within ourselves, but also we become united with God. We are our worst enemy. There cannot be any enemy outside of ourselves.

Question.—What is imagination?

Answer.—It is thought with the image in progression. In other words, it is more concrete thought than the abstract reasoning.

Question.—Does imagination make us impracticable?

Answer.—That depends upon what kind of imagination we indulge in. If the imagination is synthetic and constructive, that is, to a practical end, as we understand the word practical, it certainly makes us most practical.

Question.—To what extent does our constructive ability depend upon our imagination?

Answer.—Imagination is the motive power in our mind.

Question.—What is the difference between thought and imagination?

Answer.—It is the same thing, only the imagination is more concrete thought, that is, a thought with a picture.

Question.—What is the difference between the divine mind and the human mind?

Answer.—If the definition of mind is that which thinks, then the divine mind is only the highly conscious human mind. The mind thinks because it is subject to relative conditions. If by the word divine mind we mean the mind of God or God-mind, the Absolute, then we ought not give the attributes of mind to it. Any attribute will reduce the Absolute to the mortal or relative plane; that cannot be, since it is above all relative conditions. Then there cannot be such a thing as divine mind, as distinct from the human mind. If God can see without eyes and hear without ears, He can certainly think without mind, if it is necessary for Him to do so. The self-existent perfect God cannot have anything to think about. If anything thinks, it is our attributed qualities, not the absolute God Himself. Any quality we attribute to the Absolute reflects back on us. Therefore we see God like and in our attributed qualities. Like the sunlight passing through a colored glass, when we see the Absolute through our attributed qualities, we perceive the divine mind. It is nothing but our higher concept or consciousness of ourselves.

Question.—Is there any mind at all?

Answer.— Yes and no. In the absolute sense there is no mind. In the relative sense there is. Our mind is nothing but the action of our relative concept.

Question.—Does our mind really act?

Answer.—It does. Nothing can exist without action. Since we admit the existence of our mind in our thought, it has its action.

Question.—How does a thing that exists act?

Answer.—Existence means the act of living or being.

Question.—In that sense, can the Divine Mind exist?

Answer.—Yes. But it is not in the sense of thinking. Thinking is an action in quality. Therefore the Divine Mind does not think, if we admit its existence.

Question.—How is our mind the action of our concept?

Answer.—We have already stated that anything that exists acts. Our concept exists, therefore it acts. But our concept, being changeable, its action is also changeable. The name of this changeable action is the human mind.

Question.—What reason have we to think that this world is unreal?

Answer.—Anything permanent is real. When we see nothing is permanent in this world, we know then that it cannot be real.

Question.—If the testimony of our senses is unreliable, is it not possible that our opinion regarding this world, upon those testimonies, may be wrong?

Answer.—Yes, it is possible. But this world cannot be, as it seems to us. If the world is different from the form we see, then this particular form of the world is unreal.

Question.—What then is the real world?

Answer.—One that never changes. Since nothing is unchangeable, but the Absolute, that world cannot be anything but the Absolute.

Question.—Is there any sex in reality?

Answer.—No. The sex belongs to the world of concept. Since everything of this world is unreal, sex cannot be real. Like all other things of this relative plane sex exists only in our concept. Its relative importance is due to the value we put upon it.

Question.—Why should we rise above all sex concept in order to reach the goal of realization?

Answer.—Because from our sex concept we incur most of our desires and attachments. It is the mother passion of all other passions. These passions hold us down to this relative plane of consciousness. We will never get salvation until we have freed ourselves from the bondage of passions.

Question.—How should we elevate our sex concept?

Answer.—By giving higher attributes to it; in other words by giving spiritual quality to it.

Question.—Why is our action justified by motive?

Answer.—Our action has no significance except the interpretation we put to it. Motive is that interpretation. Without its reaction an action can have any significance to us. We regulate an action on account of its reaction upon us. According to our interpretation an action reacts upon us. For example, if we strike a ruffian in order to save a defenceless child, we do not feel the reaction, which we call remorse, on account of the interpretation we put upon our action.

Question.—To what extent is our concept responsible for the interpretation of an action?

Answer.—To a large extent. Except when we disobey the dictate of our natural concept.

Question.—Has diet anything to do with our spiritual unfoldment?

Answer.—In this world of concept everything depends upon our concept. Whatever we eat, we can make spiritual by our thought, if we want to. Hence diet has nothing to do with our spiritual unfoldment. But those who believe in dieting will have the effect therefrom. In our opinion the very importance we attach to the matter of diet makes us more self-conscious of the condition we want to overcome by dieting. We ought not to pay any attention to what and when we shall eat. When we feel hungry we ought to eat and whatever we like best, and what we think best. With the realization of this truth there comes a time in our life when we do not care what we eat.

Question.—How shall we spiritualize our food?

Answer.—By holding the thought that it is the gift of Spirit, therefore it is spiritual and wholesome.

Question.—Why does some food hurt us in spite of our good thought regarding it?

Answer.—In order to trace the cause we have to go back to the conditions which are parts of our being. These conditions constitute our being, since our concept is the sum total of them. Nothing can hurt us which has no corresponding condition or conditions within us. When our good thought regarding a food does not change our general concept, it may hurt us, if it does not agree with our nature. By thinking of food as a gift of our higher Ideal we can make it agree with us, because the quality of thought changes the concept of our being.

Question.—Why should we take no thought of our physical body?

Answer.—Because by the thought of our physical body we

94

recognize the conditions pertaining to the concept of that body. Our physical body cannot exceed in quality the conditions of our concept.

Question.—What is the physical concept?

Answer.—It is the concept of disease and death.

Question.—How can we overcome this concept?

Answer.—There is no direct way to overcome it on account of the suggestion of polar opposites. There is an indirect way, which never fails. It is to think less of ourselves and more of our Ideal, and that our Ideal has the absolute control of our being.

Question.—Why can some people not be healed?

Answer.—Some people are so constituted that they would rather die than give up their old concept of life. Their soul seems to be ossified by the material concept of life. Were they to shake off their lethargy and stand in the name of the Almighty to assert their own rights, nothing in this universe would keep them from getting well. All that they need is more air and light in their soul, in order to get well and remain well.

Question.—What is the principal point to keep in mind in Yoga healing?

Answer.—That the quality of thought changes our concept. Disease being in the concept, with its change, disease disappears, After curing many complicated diseases we are convinced, that nothing is more certain in effecting a cure than this method of healing.

Question.—Can we narrate any instances where we have made instantaneous cures?

Answer.—Yes, we can, though we do not know whether or not these cures ought to be called instantaneous. A man who did not walk without crutches for two years came one day to see us. We explained to him the philosophy of the quality of thought, and he readily grasped it. Inside of fifteen minutes he walked home without crutches. Since then he has been well. One day we were called to attend a young man who was confined to his bed for many weeks. The physicians diagnosed his case as abscess in the kidneys. We gave him only one treatment and told him to get up and dress, which he did. He has been well ever since. One treatment cured a bedridden young girl. We could cite many other cases.

Question.—What is required to be a successful healer?

Answer.—The realization of the fact that a disease exists only in one's concept, and the physical body is the outward expression of that concept. That, by changing the concept by the higher quality of thought or idea, we can cure so-called physical diseases. When one has the full grasp of this truth he can be a successful healer.

Question.—What is the principal obstacle to be a Yoga healer?

Answer.—It is the concept of the physical body as a solid mass, regulated by a physical law. With the grosser concept of the physical body we make our power of healing grosser by the quality of thought. Our concept of a certain thing carries our conviction to others by emanation.

Question.—Can we make all people receptive?

Answer.—If they are willing to conform to our instructions we can make them receptive.

Question.—How can we approach a person with this metaphysics, if he is opposed to it?

Answer.—By not introducing this metaphysics at once. At the same time we should draw such practical illustrations which will appeal to his particular concept. Then we are to tell him about the demonstrations that can be made by following the teaching of Christian Yoga.

Question.—What is the relative philosophical concept of matter?

Answer.—Matter is a part of spirit. Like the sun and its rays spirit and matter are inseparable, and both permanent. Matter, in fact, is the constant manifestation of the action of spirit. Since this action indicates the life of spirit, it never ceases to act. Every action has a reaction; the action of the spirit is constantly reacting back on Itself. This material creation is due to this reaction. As the new action is starting in every moment, so every

96

moment, Spirit is having new reaction or creation. These new reactions are causing constant change in this creation. Our physical body is supposed to be the part action of the spirit and our spirit is a part spirit of the whole.

Question.—If we are all one how can telepathic relation be established between two persons?

Answer.—Our concept sustains our individuality. The concept gives us the sense of space and duality of life. Since in reality no thought or idea can be outside of us, the real meaning of telepathy is the recognition of a thought of our own concept attributed to a different individuality, which we believe to receive through the space. With the realization of our higher concept we are able to understand the real meaning and cause of telepathy. Until we have come to the realization we have to work through the relative concept and be satisfied with the relative explanation.

Question.—Is financial demonstration a part of Yoga teaching?

Answer.—Christian Yoga lays special stress on the quality of thought. If our concept of finance is a means for physical comfort, we doubt whether anyone can profit by it. Knowing that a thing has not any quality or power except what we vest in it, we cannot rely on finance as a medium of happiness. If, by living a spiritual life and trusting in the all-provident wisdom of our Ideal, we can get whatever we wish, there is no need of our making finance a special point. A man ought not to sell his higher concept of life to the God of mammon. We ought not to forget, that fortune hardly follows those who run after it, but it always follows those who have gained mastery over it.

Question.—What is the best way to master the financial condition?

Answer.—To think as little as we can about it and to trust everything in the unerring guidance of our Ideal. To express a mere wish with the proper understanding of the law of our being is sufficient for any purpose. The only thing necessary is the understanding and trust.

97

Question.—*Why do people who are studying along this line lay special stress on the financial problem?*

Answer.—It is due to two distinct reasons. One is the popular demand of this particular age, and another may be due to limited concept of life.

Question.—*Is it not proper to teach the people first how to free themselves from the financial worry and then give them the higher spiritual teaching?*

Answer.—That purpose can be served by teaching them the right way of living. If any one demands more wealth than he needs he transgresses the law of his being; that is, he confines himself more to his limited concept of life. Greed is not the cure of poverty or poverty the cure of greed. It is the understanding of the law which makes us free from both poverty and greed. By spiritualizing the concept of wealth we learn to appreciate the true value of it.

Question.—*What is the best prayer we can offer when we are in want?*

Answer.—The Lord is my Shepherd and I shall not want.

Question.—*If we are to trust in the guidance of our Ideal for everything, what is the use of putting forth any external effort?*

Answer.—There is no need of putting forth meaningless external effort, except what is necessary in order to follow the mandate of our Ideal. If it directs us to do a certain thing we ought to do it, not as our work but as the work of our Ideal.

Question.—*How may we know that Christian Yoga is teaching the truth?*

Answer.—By referring our question to our Ideal. When we ask our Ideal to answer any question we receive the answer by waiting in silence.

Question.—*How can we realize our oneness with God?*

Answer.—By surrendering everything to Him. By giving everything to our higher Ideal we become that Ideal ourselves by the quality of thought.

Question.—*Has God intelligence like ours?*

Answer.—It has been already stated that the absolute God

98

is beyond all attributes. Intelligence is really an attribute. It is human concept of life. God has no intelligence, but when we use it in the absolute sense He is intelligence Himself.

Question.—Is there any knowlelge beyond reason?

Answer.—Certainly. Knowledge is God. Beyond human reason God exists. The reason weighs the matter of which it is doubtful, in order to arrive at a right conclusion. But knowledge is that part of our life which we know by realization. Many a time we may realize conditions or states, which we may not be able to prove by reason.

Question.—What is the reason that we feel more drawn towards one soul than another?

Answer.—It is not a soul drawn to a soul, but it is rather a concept drawn to another of a similar nature. Whenever we attribute some of our favorite qualities to a person, or the person himself manifests those qualities, we feel drawn to him.

Question.—Why do we attribute some of our favorite qualities to a certain person?

Answer.—It is because we associate those qualities with his personal appearance or form. The form which we like best on account of our inner concept suggests the possibility of its possessing our favorite qualities.

Question.—What assurance have we that we shall live after our body disintegrates?

Answer.—This question is suggestive of the relative concept of life. We know that we live because we are conscious of our existence. It makes no difference whether we live in our thought or in reality. No reason can supercede our consciousness of being. The only thing we can dispute is, whether we exist in the form we think ourselves to exist. We are discussing the question of existence not of form. The consciousness which knows that it exists, is not any quality of the so-called physical body. We know that our consciousness transcends our physical existence. Hence we never lose our consciousness that we exist.

Question.—Is our consciousness God Consciousness?

Answer.—Yes, it is.

Question.—Why then is our consciousness so limited?

Answer.—The consciousness is in itself nonqualified. But it takes the apparent qualities of our concept when it works through it. Mine, thine, yours are the qualities of our concept; above all these stands the universal Cosmic Consciousness.

Question.—Why does the universal Consciousness seem to take qualities of our relative concept?

Answer.—It may seem to take the qualities of the relative plane, but in reality it does not. The consciousness is above qualities. But when we imagine that It takes the qualities, the very imagination makes It appear so. Our consciousness is really God Consciousness, only our thought or imagination gives it the appearance of limitation. But the self-existing Consciousness can never die, because It is beyond all change, form, time, space, and condition; It is the Absolute.

Question.—What is the constant cause of worry?

Answer.—The lack of faith in the all-providing Law. It is due to the limitation we put upon ourself.

Question.—What is the cause of disease?

Answer.—The indirect answer has already been given. The cause is the stagnation or congestion in our being or concept, which is due to neglect in giving response to the change which our inner nature demands.

Question.—How can we know that we are not giving response to the demand of our inner nature?

Answer.—We can know it by the life we live. Whenever we do not follow our better understanding we fail to give response to our own nature.

Question.—What is the difference between sin and disease?

Answer.—Sin is the cause of disease. By making atonement for the sin we have committed, we become free from disease and death. We make Atonement or at-one-ment by giving ourselves to God. Because it is by giving ourselves to our higher Ideal we become one with It.

Question.—Is it desirable to form a strong attachment for a being or a condition?

Answer.—No, from attachment comes all misery. By giving ourselves and all our desired objects to our Lord God we become free from attachment.

Question.—Is there such a thing as fate?

Answer.—Yes, and no. We are the architects of our fate. By living a certain way we create a certain condition within us. The sum total of these conditions largely determines our future.

Question.—If it is not due to fate or predestination how can a person foresee what is going to happen to others?

Answer.—Any sensitive person can almost sense the inner conditions of those who come near him. From the impression of the sum total of their past and present conditions he can intuitively feel, where they are going to be led, if they continue their old life. It is like the headlight of an automobile, which throws light ahead of it in a certain direction. When it is coming in a certain direction we can see everything ahead of it and whither it is bound for. But if it suddenly changes its course our prediction will not come true. Fore-telling is the logical deduction of fore-glimpse from one's past and present conditions.

Question.—What is the highest and best life we can live in this plane?

Answer.—It is the life of self denial and the surrender of ourselves to our highest Ideal. When we give our troubles, cares, and worries, pains, aches, misery, poverty, sin and death to our immortal all-powerful Ideal, we become free from the bondage of limitation. By giving our limited concept we gain eternal life. That is the only way and that is the only life.

The Light of the World

"That ye may be the children of your Father which is in heaven; he maketh his sun to rise on the evil and on the good, sendeth rain on the just and on the unjust." "Be ye therefore perfect, even as your Father which is in heaven is perfect."

We cannot possibly hope to understand the teaching of the Master if we do not understand his concept of life. He tried to explain his concept of life, both by his words and deeds. He discovered that in this vast ocean of life, humanity holds the concept of non-life. In spite of this misconcept the eternal consciousness is manifesting through our consciousness of self-existence. Where is there a man, who does not believe in his own existence? To ask the question, whether we exist or not, is to admit that we exist. That which asks a question exists before the question is asked. This consciousness of self-existence is a self-evident fact, and needs no proof. The Master discovered that it was not the question of existence, but the concept of that existence, which was of vast importance and which had the great bearing upon our life. That which exists is the absolute eternal God. Our existence is in this sense, God's existence. But yet in our concept we are so far removed from that consciousness that we do not know ourselves as we are. We exist in God-Life, that is, we live God-Life in our limited concept. The difference between man and God is only in the concept. This concept makes a man, man, and God, God. Hence man is not God. Man is the limited consciousness of God. That does not mean God is limited in his consciousness, it simply means God consciousness is expressed through the limited concept, which we call man. What we think and are conscious of, that we are. What we think ourselves to be, creates us in the quality of that thought. This thought creation will always be a limited creation until we have come to the realization of our divine oneness. When we become as one with the Father we will cease to create our self and let the

Father's will be done. When we exist in God consciousness as God consciousness, we cease to exist as a human being. In that day of resurrection and restoration to the full life of consciousness, we are transformed into the Divine Being.

Master Jesus realized that before we come to the Divine Consciousness we must be children of our Father in our consciousness. Our consciousness of our own individuality is the child of that Great Cosmic Consciousness. But in order to understand this we must come to the consciousness of the fatherhood of God. As the father reproduces himself in the form of his child, so the great Cosmic Consciousness appears through our concept. Therefore our consciousness is the reproduction or image of the Divine consciousness through our concept. The more we give ourselves to our Father the more of the Father's consciousness we receive. When we return to our Father, like the prodigal son, He takes us back and makes us heir to his Divine Consciousness. The very thought that we are children of our Father and He is taking care of our burdens and cares, gives us greater assurance and higher concept of life. The Master knew that all the diseases flesh or limited concept is heir to, can be remedied by changing one's concept for a higher Ideal. By the power of his divine consciousness he cast out devils, the old morbid concepts of life. He certainly taught his disciples how to. heal all the ailments of the world. There is but one panacea for all ailments, that is to raise a man to the height of divine concept. The Master never recognized disease, either of physical or so-called mental origin, because he knew that man exists as a whole of his concept, not as a part. When we see a man, we see him as a whole. Internally and externally he is the same individuality. Consequently when the Master saw a man afflicted in part He treated the whole man. A man's consciousness is indivisible and a disease exists in his consciousness. Therefore part affliction in a man means the whole affliction. Since a disease and its effect cannot exist, if one is not conscious of it, the consciousness is responsible for the existence of a disease. The Master knew full well that there is but one disease in man and one remedy for it. The limited concept is his disease and its remedy is the atonement or the realization of Divine oneness. All the different diseases are the various expressions of one disease which is chronic in man of flesh, or limited concept. When we cure an expression or a form of a disease, we do not cure the disease itself. Only by inculcating the divine wisdom in a man and elevating his concept of life, can we cure disease. By curing one form or expression of disease, we leave a man exposed to the attack of another. Therefore such method of healing which inculcates the divine wisdom in man and changes the very concept of his being for better, is entitled to the name divine healing. Divine healing does not mean to use divine power in healing alone, it also means to give a person divine concept in order to cure his limited concept. The Master Jesus never healed a physical disease, because he did not believe in it. He healed a man of his spiritual inertia. He made a man whole in his concept. When a man is whole in his concept he is whole as a man. When he rebuked the multitude for their lack of faith and right concept of life, he always had in mind their limited concept of life. To the extent he succeeded in changing a man into the new life, he was successful in healing his ailment. The new life means the new or higher concept of life. This concept does not mean the mere momentary, impulsive sentiment or an intellectual grasp of the philosophical discourse of life, it means the vital realization of God's presence in one's soul. It is the very God consciousness we so often speak of. God consciousness is not really very far from our individual consciousness. As we are conscious of our own existence, so we can be conscious of God's presence in our consciousness. By adding God, our higher concept of life, to our consciousness, we can have the realization of the God consciousness. Yet those who are far away from God in their concept, never find God in the whole universe. Some people, not understanding the law of being, think that the great illumination, or Divine consciousness, comes like a bright, dazzling light, which the eyes of ordinary mortals cannot endure. When we have the illumination, or come to know the truth, we do not notice any dazzling light, we simply become conscious of the divine presence. Illumination means the higher consciousness. Some people manifest a certain amount of power and call it Divine power. It may be the manifestation of Divine power, but it may not be the illumination of Divine Consciousness. Coming to the new light or truth does not mean the intellectual comprehension of the truth, it means the realization. When a man realizes the truth as the Master taught, he does not feel the necessity of doing anything for himself any longer; he lets the Truth do everything for him. He does not rely any more on the external means and ways, because he knows full well that all things work together for our good and are regulated by an invisible law. The law knows our wants and supplies them according to our need. Therefore he is always calm and peaceful. In a degree we lose the hold on the Truth do we worry and fear. Do you not know what the Master said? *"Which of you by taking thought can add one cubit unto his stature?"* What the Master meant is, that by taking any thought of ourselves by our limited concept we cannot do any more than our concept permits us. When we know that there is a power, greater than we have yet realized, and that power is the sole master of our being, we can perform wonders in the name and with the consciousness of that power. Master Jesus always praised God and gave all the credit to Him for what He did in His name. By so doing He gained the very consciousness which He constantly kept before His mind. Then came the time in His life when He was totally merged in the Divine Consciousness. That is the time He claimed that who had seen Him had seen His Father. The keynote of His whole teaching is, that by the constant thought of our Ideal we become that Ideal. Not only the thought of our Ideal, but any thought, if we hold it constantly in our minds will change us into its quality. If we hate anything for any length of time we become hateful ourselves. So the thought that our Ideal is within us and acting through us is the nearest road to the greater consciousness. Our limited concept is like a habit, we have to overcome it by establishing another concept. When we put forth direct effort to change our concept, we have hardly any chance

105

to succeed, because we take more of the condition or nature of a thought we are conscious of. The Master Jesus knew it, and therefore he showed us the direct and nearest road to the goal of realization. A thought without quality is non-productive. As we think so we become does not mean, that a thought without its quality can change us. The ideal quality of thought transforms us into that ideal. The Master's disciples made Him their Ideal and gave everything to Him, they in return gained the Master's life and became like Him in consciousness. Therefore, He said, *"Give and it shall be given unto you, for the same measure that ye mete withal it shall be measured to you again."* Then again He said, *"The disciple is not above his Master, but everyone that is perfect shall be as his Master."* By this statement He tried to convey that we cannot go beyond our Ideal, but we can be as perfect as our Ideal. When He said *"Be ye therefore perfect, even as your Father which is in Heaven is perfect,"* He showed us the still greater possibility of our unfoldment. When a man realizes the Divine Consciousness within him he knows that everything is possible with that Consciousness. The very vortex which is supposed to hold a thing together exists in that conscious power. Therefore with the realization of the Divine Consciousness, when we wish anything our desire is fulfilled. He said, *"For verily I say unto you, that whosoever shall say unto this mountain, be thou removed, and be thou cast into the sea; and shall not doubt in his heart, but shall believe that those things he saith shall come to pass; he shall have whatsoever he saith."* Without the Divine Consciousness we cannot have such faith in ourselves. When we understand and realize that a vortex of a thing is our concept and that concept is in Divine Consciousness we simply have a glimpse of the truth, which the Master taught and preached. From the height of Divine Consciousness, when we command the deadly poison to have no effect on us it loses its effect. Because the higher concept of life changes the very root of our being. The being which is subject to poison, disease, and death exists no more. It is God Almighty's life which commands all things of this ephemeral world, to obey its mandate and they

106

obey, because the things of the ephemeral world cannot rise above their creator. God being the only life, the world of concept exists only in name, for that which is eternal and immortal. From the height of the spiritual concept, when we survey the whole creation of death and mortality we understand how things can obey our mandate.

The Master Jesus taught his disciples and followers to always keep the highest Ideal condition before them; because that is the only way to salvation. He said to his followers, *"Bless them that curse you and pray for them that despitefully use you."* Then he said, *"Be ye therefore merciful, as your Father also is merciful."* His concept of Father is so high and elevated and soul inspiring that none but those who are initiated into the mystery of life are able to understand it. It is not a father who is far away from his son, but it is a Father who is the Life of our lives. That Divine consciousness whose little ray is coming through our miscalled and misconceived life and individuality is our real Father. When we establish unity with the Father by widening our consciousness we abide in peace, trust, and harmony. It makes no difference who we are, and what kind of life we have lived, once we wake up to the consciousness of Divine Power within us our salvation is assured. According to the Master, when a man repents, that is, when he changes his past concept of life into a new concept, he goes to heaven. The Master said to those who still held to the old concept of life, *"Verily I say unto you, That the publicans and the harlots go into the kingdom of God before you."* The Kingdom of God, the higher inner consciousness, where peace, harmony and love abide, is within man. A man without changing his old life for the new cannot retire within. That unruffled condition where the higher consciousness dwells is our real within. The Master said: *"But seek ye first the kingdom of God, and his righteousness; and all these things shall be added unto you."* Through realization we reach that state of calmness and peace which is called the Kingdom of God. In this Kingdom all our desires are fulfilled. He again said: *"Therefore I say unto you, take no thought for your life, what ye shall eat, or what ye shall drink, nor yet for your body, what ye shall put on. Is not the life more than meat, and the body than raiment?"* Why did he say that? Because by the thought of all these things we absorb the quality of the thought and avoid the life of trust, peace and happiness. By relying on our Ideal and living the life we elevate our concept or consciousness. By taking thought of the earthly things we cannot make them come our way without following the law of our being. Our life is regulated by that law; and everything pertaining to this life likewise is subject to the same law. When we consciously or unconsciously create a condition for a thing it will come to us. The right way to create the condition for a thing is to trust in the great law of supply. What a wonderful significance the word trust has! A man who had been given up by the regular physicians and whose death was momentarily expected was saved by that one concept, trust in the decision of the Almighty. You may call it suggestion if you want to, it makes very little difference as far as the great law is concerned. When this life is given into the hand of the Almighty, it is protected. There cannot be anything called half trust. When we trust our life in the hand of that Great Life we do not care whether we live or die. Because to trust in the immortal life is to be immortal. Does the fish worry about the water when it lives in the ocean? Why do not the people understand this simple law. If your suggestion for health gives you health, as you believe it will, why will not your suggestion for the greater life and consciousness give you the greater life and consciousness. The greater consciousness exists, because we attain to it. We also know it has the greater power and efficiency, than we ordinarily command, because we have many evidences to that effect. When we know that our consciousness of ourselves is very limited and we are constantly conscious of that limitation, why should we not resort to such means which assure more life to us, and which also mean greater efficiency and power to materialize such conditions as we may desire, according to our ever growing consciousness. Without the consciousness this life will have no significance. No matter what

108

it is, that which gives us higher and higher consciousness is our religion. If we want the realization we must put aside foolish pride of earthly position, education, and wisdom. When we are divinely inspired we can have wisdom and knowledge which no earthly academy can ever teach us. The Godly man receives a different kind of education. He receives this education in the Kingdom of God and direct from the Almighty. Yes; God Almighty teaches us the great lessons of life through inspiration and spiritual illumination. We must first be like little children if we want to enter into the Kingdom of God. The Master said: *"Verily I say unto you, whosoever shall not receive the Kingdom of God as a little child shall in no wise enter therein."* He again said: *"Suffer little children to come unto me, and forbid them not; for of such is the Kingdom of God."* How simple is the solution of this life, yet so far away from the concept of those who are still in the dense fog of maya or illusion. The simplicity of a child's faith works wonders. A man who was in a terrific cyclone, which demolished several sea coast cities, and caused several thousand people to lose their lives, remembered the injunction of his spiritual teacher, that whoever trusts in the great protecting power of this universe in time of danger, is always protected. In spite of the great fury of the cyclone and wrecks all around him, he was led to a place of safety in a semi-conscious state. The next morning when he woke up from his trance condition he found himself so far away from the place where he lived that he could hardly come back through the heaps of debris without the help of assistance. He came across another wonderful case of delivery immediately after this cyclone. When he went to an island about forty miles from the coast with the relief corps, he saw a little boy of four who was carried away sixteen miles over the sea from one island to another by the waves which overrun the island, where thousands found a watery grave. How the little child was saved was long the question of speculation. It simply goes to prove that in this relative conscious plane there exists a law of our being. Whatever happens to us is in response to the inner conditions which we create within us. By changing our so-called concept we can either change the happenings or their influence over us. Physical death may approach a man in response to the inner conditions of his being, but if he knows the law he can overcome death by changing the very concept of life wherein lie the conditions. So we can defy disease and death by giving ourselves to our higher concept of life. We know that sometimes things happen to us which we do not expect. This is due to our inner conditions, which we create by the way we live and think. We have seen men travel through the forest with the absolute trust in God, being never molested by the beasts of prey. But those who go through the same place relying upon their firearms are often in danger of their lives. How wonderful is the invisible conscious plane!

The Master, Jesus, made one of the great metaphysical statements when he said: *"And when ye stand praying, forgive, if ye have aught against any: that your Father also which is in Heaven may forgive your trespasses."* Now the question is, why will it be necessary to forgive when we are praying? The great mystery of life is unity. All lives are one. In the degree we understand this truth do we understand the meaning of the prayer. Upon our understanding of the meaning of prayer depends its answer. If we want our prayer answered, we must first establish the unity with the great Life, God. God-life being the only life, our lives are also God-life. Consequently if we are not in harmony with anyone, we cannot be in harmony with God. To forgive is to establish harmony or unity. When we establish unity with a person with whom we have no unity, God, our heavenly Father, establishes unity with us. Therefore the Master said: *"But if ye do not forgive, neither will your Father which is in Heaven forgive your trespasses."* Our trespasses or sins are our limited concept, and it works against our better understanding, which detach our consciousness from God. The Master was very forgiving. He was ready to forgive even the worst sinners. Students of the Bible will remember the passage where the scribes and Pharisees brought to him the woman taken in adultery. The Master said to them who brought the woman before him: *"He*

110

that is without sin among you, let him first cast a stone at her." But none dared do it, and, feeling guilty in their conscience, they departed one by one. When the Master had lifted up Himself and saw none but the woman, he said to her: *"Woman, where are those thine accusers? Hath no man condemned thee?"* She said, *"No man, Lord."* And Jesus said to her: *"Neither do I condemn thee; go and sin no more."* The Master condemned very strongly the fault-finding spirit. He knew that it lowers a man's moral nature or concept and distracts his attention from the spiritual concept of life. Therefore He said: *"Why beholdest thou the mote that is in thy brother's eye, but perceivest not the beam that is in thine own eye? Either how canst thou say to thy brother, Brother, let me pull out the mote that is in thine eye, when thou thyself beholdest not the beam that is in thine own eye? Thou hypocrite, cast out first the beam out of thine own eye, and than shalt thou see clearly to pull out the mote that is in thy brother's eye."*

Jesus certainly showed the way to the full life. He showed the road of perfect trust, love and forgiveness. Instead of denying us the same divine rights and origin which he claimed for himself, he confirmed it. Some of his utterances were made from the lofty heights of spiritual realization. Therefore those who were not within, to quote the Master's words, could not comprehend the meaning when he said: *"I am the light of the world: he that followeth me shall not walk in darkness, but shall have the light of life."* What a grand realization the Master had, *"I am the light of the world."* Why should he not be the light of the world, when he claimed to be at one with the Father? A man who can lose himself entirely in the ocean of Divine Consciousness cannot exist any more as a man. He is certainly the light, or the example of the world. Did he not tell us, *"When ye have lifted up the Son of man, then shall ye know that I am he, and that I do nothing of myself; but as my Father hath taught me, I speak these things."* Oh, what a grand concept! Can there be anything more soul-inspiring than this? Think of the great spiritual truth, that when we have lifted up the Son of man—that is, the concept of the son of man, or flesh—then shall we know that he, the concept above the Son of man, is the Christ, our Savior, the Divine Consciousness. Then he says that he does nothing of himself, but as his Father, his Divine Consciousness, has taught him, he speaks all these things. Here the man Jesus is crucified and the Divine Jesus rises in perfect glory to Divine Consciousness. When the Pharisees said to Him, *"Thou bearest record of thyself; thy record is not true,"* the Master answered and said to them, *"Though I bear record of myself, yet my record is true, for I know whence I came, and whither I go; but ye cannot tell whence I come, and whither I go." "Ye judge after the flesh; I judge no man. And yet if I judge, my judgment is true; for I am not alone, but I and the Father that sent me. It is also written in your law that the testimony of two men is true. I am one, bear witness of myself, and the Father that sent me beareth witness of me."* When the Master said that *"Ye judge after the flesh"* he meant according to the limited concept, but *"I judge no man."* He meant He did not judge anybody as a man, but as an expression of God, or of God Consciousness. Yet if he would judge his judgment would be true, because, He being with God, or having the realization of God-Consciousness, understood the true nature of man. Man has no consciousness except what he borrows from God and expresses through his limited concept, *"I am one, bear witness of myself,"* that is, bear witness that I and my Father are one. My Father, the Divine Consciousness, whom I am manifesting now, bears witness of myself. Then they asked, *"Where is Thy Father?"* Jesus answered, *"Ye neither know me, nor my Father: If ye had known me, ye should have known my Father also." "I being as one with my Father, you would have known Him had you known me."* Then Jesus said again to them: *"Ye are from beneath; I am from above; ye are from of this world; I am not of this world."* You maintain your existence from your earthly concept of life, and I maintain mine from Cosmic Concept. You belong to this world of limitation, but I do not. Then Jesus said to them: *"If God is your Father, ye would love me: for I proceeded forth and came from God; neither*

112

came I of myself, but He sent me. Why do ye not understand my speech? Even because ye cannot hear my word."

Among many other statements of the Master the following are of deep interest: *"Therefore doth my Father love me, because I lay down my life, that I might take it again."*

"The works that I do in my Father's name, they bear witness of me."

"I and my Father are one."

"Many good works have I shown you from my Father; for which of those works de ye stone me?" The Jews answered him saying, *"For a good work we stone thee not; but for blasphemy; and because that thou, being a man, makest thyself God."*

Jesus answered them, *"Is it not written in your law, I said, Ye are Gods? If he called them Gods, unto whom the word of God came, and the scripture cannot be broken; Say ye of him, whom the Father hath sanctified, and sent into the world, Thou blasphemest; because I said, I am the son of God? If I do not the works of my Father, believe me not. But if I do, though ye believe not me, believe the works; that ye may know, and believe, that the Father is in me, and I in Him."*

In another place he said to his disciples: *"A new commandment I give unto you, That ye love one another; as I have loved you, that ye also love one another."* It expressed the great love of the Master for his disciples. He wants them to establish the same unity with one another as he did with them. He loved them and they loved him. In this new commandment he wants them to see his spirit in one another. The spirit which means the unity with God is the spirit of the Master. He wanted them all to realize that spirit among themselves.

Now the question is what Jesus meant by the word death. If we are all of God and from God we cannot die. The eternal immortal principle in a man never dies. What does die then? It is the concept that gives rise to mine, thine and yours; in other words, the concept of separate life from God. That which gives the eternal consciousness the appearance of mortal or changeable being cannot exist in sin or limitation, which is transitory and

113

which is not real. This concept, or life of sin cannot have God Consciousness because it opposes the unity with God. The Master said, *"I go my way, and ye shall seek me, and shall die in your sin; whither I go, ye cannot come."* It means I lead my own life according to my realization, and you may seek me or my consciousness, but you cannot come there with your transitory concept of life. You, as you understand yourself to be, will die or come to an end in your concept of limitation or sin. Man can never exist without God. The Godless concept is without God or God Life. Therefore it cannot exist. Neither can It reach God or God Consciousness when its condition is against that Consciousness. Therefore the Master said, *"Ye are of your father the devil, and lusts of your father ye will do. He was a murderer from the beginning, and abode not in the truth, because there is no truth in him. When he speaketh a lie, he speaketh of his own: for he is a liar, and the father of it. And because I tell you the truth, ye believe me not. Which of you convinceth me of sin? And if I say the truth, why do ye not believe me? He that is of God heareth God's words; ye therefore hear them not, because ye are not of God."* All this time the Master was speaking of their concept, which is false and untruthful and which they think they themselves are. Their limited concept is born of the limited concept; that is to say, a limited concept or idea produces a limited result. As long as humanity will try to see the limitless God with their Godless concept, so long they will never see God in their consciousness. The Master had the highest concept of God. It was an impersonal, immanent God. The Master said, *"I seek not mine own glory; there is one that seeketh and judgeth. Verily, verily, I say unto you, if a man keep my saying, he shall never see death."* That is, when a man observes or lives according to his saying he will never have that detachment or stagnant condition which is called death. When our concept is Godless and inharmonious we invite death. Jesus said, *"If I honour myself, my honour is nothing; it is my Father that honoureth me; of whom ye say, that He is your God. Yet ye have not known him; but I know him: and if I should say, I*

114

know him not, I shall be a liar like unto you: I know him, and keep his sayings. Verily, verily, I say unto you, before Abraham was, I am." This last sentence is fraught with deep meaning. The "I am" or "I consciousness" always exists. It existed before Abraham, nay, before everything else. It is God. The Master Jesus made this statement from his Cosmic Consciousness. It seems as though he lived in a dual concept, the Son and the Father. Therefore, sometimes he would speak as Father, sometimes as his Son. The difference between the two concepts is not very great. They say there are many contradictions in the Master's sayings. If they will take them from different view points, such as Son and Father, they will find no contradictions whatever. As a Son he spoke as it became a son, but when he spoke as the Father, he assumed all the dignity of the Father. How marvelous is the inner plane of consciousness. Judging from reason or from cause to effect, we do not at all understand the great mystery of this life. Only by realization do we understand the great mystery of life. By symbolical language we try to introduce the great spiritual truth, but the truth always remains unexpressed to those who have not the realization.

It has been already stated that the difference between the Master's concepts of Father and Son is not very great, except when he made reference to the son of man. He said, *"My Father worketh hitherto, and I work. Verily, verily, I say unto you, the Son can do nothing of himself, but what he seeth the Father do: for what things soever he doeth, these also doeth the Son likewise. For the Father loveth the Son, and showeth him all things that himself doeth: and he will show him greater work than these, that ye may marvel. For as the Father raiseth up the dead, and quickeneth them; even so the Son quickeneth whom he will."*

Then again he said: *"Verily, verily, I say unto you, he that heareth my word, and believeth on Him that sent me, hath everlasting life, and shall not come to condemnation; but is passed from death unto life."* It means who hears his word in his spiritual concept and believes in the great Cosmic Consciousness,

115

he will have everlasting life or concept. He will be passed from the Godless mortal concept to the eternal concept of life.

Then he said, *"Verily, verily, I say unto you, the hour is coming, and now is, when the dead shall hear the voice of the Son of God: and they that hear shall live. For as the Father hath life in himself, so hath he given to the Son to have life in himself; and given authority to execute judgment also, because he is the Son of man."* He has used the terms Son of man and Son of God. There is a great difference between the two concepts; one is the Son of limited consciousness and the other is the Son of Divine Consciousness. When we have lifted up the Son of man he becomes the Son of God, Christ. The Son of man uses his judgment and will. But the Son of God lets the Father do everything for him or he does as his Father directs him to do. When we come down from our God-Consciousness we become the son of man again. This is not the state of perfect everlasting unity. When the Master was speaking of going to his Father for all time he was referring to the everlasting unity, or Divine-Consciousness. One realizing the condition of Son of God, when we come back to the state of son of man, we are not the same man any more. We carry with us the pleasant memory of our experience and it makes us a new being.

When the Master said, that the time was coming when the dead should hear the voice of the Son of God, he meant the dead or those devoid of spiritual concept would have the spiritual concept. Having gained that concept they would live or have the concept of life. Speaking about the judgment the Master said: *"I can of mine own self do nothing: as I hear I judge; and my judgment is just; because I seek not mine own will, but the will of the Father which hath sent me."* This will explain the following: *"For the Father judgeth no man, but hath committed all judgment unto the Son."* Since the Father is perfect he has nothing to judge. But the Son seeks the knowledge to judge the condition which is helpful for the perfect unity with the Father. The Father gives what the Son desires, trusting in his power of giving. Therefore the Master said: *"Ask, and it*

116

shall be given you; seek, and ye shall find; knock, and it shall be opened unto you. For everyone that asketh receiveth; and he that seeketh findeth; and to him that knocketh it shall be opened. Or, what man is there of you, whom if his son ask bread, will give him a stone? If ye, then, being evil, know how to give good gifts unto your children, how much more shall your Father which is in heaven give goods things to them that ask him."

What did the Master mean when he said: *"I seek not mine own will, but the will of the Father which hath sent me."* Why did the Master lay so little stress on the personal will? Because the Master knew full well that a man's will cannot exceed his own concept. The concept which suggests nothing but limitation cannot give a man the realization of his unlimited power. For example, if we tell a man that by exercising his will he can demonstrate whatever he wants to, that will not give him the power to exercise his will more than his limited concept permits. The man who has lived all his life with the concept of limitation cannot easily forget his limitation. The very affirmation for the limitless strength is liable to make him conscious of his limitation. The Master knew when we do things according to the will of the limitless Father we have no reason to think of our limitation. Consequently our action oversteps the bound of our limited concept of will. The human will, like his concept, cannot bring full response from Cosmic Life. But when he places himself under the guidance of that Life his own personal will is submerged by it. The centre of our personal will is very small and the jurisdiction it covers is also very limited. When the human mind merges into Divine Consciousness it exercises the Divine will. Not that the Divine will, like the personal will, needs to put forth any effort, but that it acts in response to our inner demand, which we make, trusting in the decision of Divine power. In other words, by the quality of thought we make that will manifest through us. For example, when we put anything near the heat, according to its power of absorbtion, it will absorb heat and make it its own. So by giving ourselves to God we make the Divine will our own. Whatever we ask of the Divine Power we

117

receive. That does not mean our mere asking will bring response from It. It depends upon how we ask. It means that we must ask with perfect understanding, that we are asking from a source that can supply our demands. The simple faith or the understanding of the operation of the law is the real secret of asking. In other words, we receive according to the spirit in which we ask.

The Master said: *"Therefore all things whatsoever ye would that a man should do to you, do ye even so to them: for this is the law and the prophets."* It also explains the spirit of our asking. The manner of asking justifies its response. In everything in our life that law is applicable. By the light of this law we can foretell the outcome of a venture. Therefore it is the prophet of our actions.

How we are able to know everything by following the truth is well illustrated by the life of the Master Jesus. When he displayed the great wisdom the people were astonished and said: *"How knoweth this man letters, having never learned?"* The Master answered them and said: *"My doctrine is not mine, but his that sent me. If any man will do his will he shall know of the doctrine, whether it be of God, or whether I speak of myself. He that speaketh of himself seeketh his own glory; but he that seeketh his glory that sent him, the same is true, and no unrighteousness is in him."* When we understand the Master's life we will see its grandeur and beauty. What a deep mystery is hidden in his teaching. It is so simple, yet so difficult to understand in the light of the world by wisdom. Unless we become like simple children or we are born again in spirit or spiritual concept we cannot understand his teaching. Without living the Master's life, even for a short duration we cannot understand the inner depth of his Divine nature. The keynote of his whole teaching is to trust and surrender ourselves to the great Cosmic Life. According to his teaching, it is by giving our smaller life we receive the greater life. Whatever we do ourselves, depending upon our limited concept, is limited. Therefore by denying or affirming a thing or a condition we cannot go beyond our

118

concept. Whatever we make and unmake by our personal effort is within that limitation. But the concept which widens the scope of our soul and brings us in touch with the Cosmic Life is the concept of our Master. When with the proper understanding of this teaching we rise to the dignity of a Divine Being, we drop all earthly conditions. We become new creatures by changing our old life. Therefore the Master said: *"Verily, verily, I say unto thee, except a man be born again, he cannot see the kingdom of God."* In order to attain to that state of perfect trust and peace we must be like little children. Therefore, He said: *"Verily, verily, I say unto you, except ye be converted, and become as little children, ye shall not enter into the Kingdom of Heaven."*

Again He said: *"That which is born of flesh is flesh; that which is born of the spirit is spirit. Marvel not that I said unto thee, 'Ye must be born again.'"* It means that which is born of the limited concept is always limited, but that which is born of the unlimited concept of spirit is unlimited. Consequently we must be born again in spiritual concept. Nothing but the concept of a boundless immanent God can ever remedy the disease of worldliness and set us free from the bondage of limitation and death. Let us remember that the Master said: *"Be ye therefore perfect, even as your Father which is in heaven is perfect."* Amen.

From The Absolute to The Relative

That which is never born and never dies, but always exists, is the Absolute, God.

He is eternal, omnipresent, and All in All. Yet He is beyond space, time, condition, change, name and form. He is the Absolute.

That which always is and All In All, cannot be more or less. That which is beyond time and space exists only in the present.

(Comment: There is no past and future in the absolute sense. All eternity, if we allow such a term, exists only in the present. The past and the future indicate time; but the present is an absolute statement, which has no significance relative to time. In the relative sense we use the term present as a point of time between the past and the future. But there is no such point possible in time, since the future always turns into the past. Therefore present is an absolute statement.)

That which exists is God. Therefore nothing can exist which is not God. The thing which is without beginning and end exists only in the absolute permanent sense; for nothing can exist which never was and never will be even in the relative sense.

If we exist now, we existed before. If we exist at all we exist as God, the Absolute and Eternal, in principle and in essence. If we exist in name, we do not exist in reality. But the thing which does not exist does not require any denial. Therefore if we have to deny our existence, we must admit that either we exist as Absolute or in name.

That which denys or approves, exists, even though it may deny or approve itself. Therefore we cannot deny our own existence. But that which is denied or approved is unreal either in statement or as a substance.

(Comment: When we deny our own existence we make an unreal statement. Because that which denies, exists before it denies anything. It cannot deny anything if it does not exist. But when we deny something else apart from ourselves it does not exist in substance, but in name, because there cannot exist more than one thing in the absolute sense. Since we cannot deny anything without admitting its existence, when we deny an unreal thing we admit at first its existence in name.)

Existence of God cannot be proved as a separate entity from ourselves. Because anything outside of ourselves cannot be proved as real. The thing which needs to be proved cannot be self-existent. That which always exists without any beginning and end only is real.

That which is conscious of its own being is real, because it is self-evident. That which is self-evident is God. Therefore our consciousness of being is God consciousness. Hence we and our God are one in the Absolute.

That which exists is one. Therefore nothing can exist which is not one. If we believe that the things around us exist, then they must exist as one.

We always deny or affirm certain conditions, but not the real substance. The conditions are no attributes of the substance, but they are our own creations through imagination. In other words, they are the imaginary values we put upon the real substance.

It is the value we attach to a thing which affects us, but not the thing itself.

(Comment: The relative value of gold, silver, copper, iron, etc., are fair examples. It is the imaginary value that causes the substance to appear as a thing. Since the value is imaginary, the thing with which we relate ourselves and which affects us is also imaginary. As a substance that thing exists, but as a value it does not. Hence a conditional existence is equal to no existence. Because it is not real.)

We always create a thing or a condition by the imagination. Anything that needs to be created, or is created is not real and self-existent. It does not exist in the absolute sense. Because a thing which has a beginning must have an end. A created thing has its beginning, therefore it cannot be permanent and real.

If this universe is created it cannot be real. But if this universe exists as an essence of God Himself it is real. This will be self-evident because it exists as One with God. The universe which we see around us changes, therefore it cannot be real, since all changeable things are unreal. But if it is a mere imaginary value of the real substance then it is our own creation. We will never see the real universe until we are acquainted with our real Self. This conditional universe is the product of the value we attach to it. The sun, moon, stars, men, women, animals, and trees are our own creations in the sense as we see them. In the absolute sense they all exist as One. They are One.

(Comment: Now the question is how the things which

do not really exist can exist in One and are One. If they do not exist as real they certainly exist as unreal. Even the very unreal thing must stand for something which is real. If an unreal thing is a mere imaginary quality or attribute, it must be the attribute we give to some thing which is real. An attribute may be wrong but it cannot change the substance to which we give that attribute. The right or wrong attribute must exist for a thing it stands for. Hence all attributes or things exist for the one real substance. Since they stand for one thing they are one in meaning and importance.)

By coming to know our own self we know the true nature of this universe. Because our self-conscious self is at one with that which is self-existent.

Different people have different impressions regarding the things they see, because they attach different values to them.

The things which our own imagination creates, our own imagination destroys. Our like and dislike, love and hate are nothing but our own creation. We create these conditions just in image of ourselves or our concept. In other words we create them just as we are.

We are what we imagine ourselves to be. This is our conditional existence, therefore it is not real. Our imaginary self enjoys, suffers, loves and hates, creates and destroys, but our real Self is above all these relative conditions.

This imagination or self creative power can only be overcome by imagination of higher quality. By the imagination that the absolute God exists in us, we come to realize Him by the quality of thought or imagination. By the law of association we absorb the quality of a thought.

Health and disease, happiness and misery all belong to our conditional or created self. The condition of health or disease corresponds to the condition of our non-self. By holding the imagination of the real Self we change our non-self and free ourselves from the bondage of conditions. We change one condition for another by the help of imagination.

If we admit that God is Omnipresent we cannot think or imagine anything beyond Him. We cannot go beyond the universal God, even the one of our relative concept.

If God is all in all he is what we believe Him to be. Yet in the absolute sense He is not what we think Him to be. Since we cannot think of any thing, which does not stand for Him, whatever we think of Him He is that. Even the wrong attribute represents the thing for which it stands. Hence our concept of God, no matter what is, indicates that which is beyond all concept.

Our attribute of a thing never can exceed our understanding or comprehension. If our understanding is imperfect, our attributes cannot be perfect. In the absolute sense there is no such state called perfect, because the thing which is beyond all qualification, cannot have a relative attribute. Hence we will never be able to give a perfect attribute to that which is self-existent. Our comprehension of the Absolute means our being Absolute. When we become one with God then we will reach a state beyond all attributes. That which exists beyond all perfections and imperfections is beyond all attributes.

Whenever we give any attribute to God we limit Him. Because our very attribute of the Infinite is after all finite, since no finite being can comprehend the Infinite. God is beyond all attributes, time, space, and condition; He is the essence and He is that which always exists.

124

By whatever name we call God, He is that. If we call Him father, mother, brother, sister or friend He becomes that to us. He is the sum total of all that exists even in the relative sense.

(Comment: Those who cannot think of God as their Self of selves, may come nearer to Him in concept by establishing some relation with Him which finds ready response from their heart. God, our own real Self reveals Himself to us in the form or attribute we want to see Him. Since all forms, as they appear before us, are our attributed qualities, to something that exists, God appears before us in the forms of our attributed qualities.)

Since, logically two things cannot occupy the same space, some people take this visible universe to be God or co-existent with God. But this visible universe exists conditionally, therefore it cannot exist in reality. The attributes which make a thing appear as we see it, are the product of our imagination. Hence they are not real. Consequently this visible universe is neither God nor part of Him.

(Comment: By the attributes we describe or limit that which is beyond all relative condition or that which is Absolute. The Absolute is the only real. By the attributes we try to qualify or explain that which is self-evident. The thing which never was, cannot be. If we grant that it existed in the essence but not in the form, we must admit that that form once was not, hence that form is impermanent, and unreal in the absolute sense. Then if this universe of form is unreal it cannot be God, since no two things can occupy the same space. Consequently this universe is neither God nor part of God, nor can it be co-existent with Him.)

What is form then? It is the attribute of that which is beyond all attributes.

(Comment: As by lines we describe figures in space so by the attributes we describe forms or things in God. As lines are not space, so attributes are not God. The real definition of a form is the supposed limitation by condition of that which is limitless. Since a condition is not a thing, but a state, the limitless God is not really limited. The space which is apparently walled in is after all free. Even in the very wall the space exists. So it is in the case of God. He exists even in the conditions which are the supposed limitations of Himself. Therefore, no matter in what condition or form we want to see God we see Him.)

They say we exist in God. If we exist at all we must be the Absolute God in the Absolute sense. We can neither be a part nor created, because that which exists always exists without any change or qualification. But when we say we exist we mean that we conditionally exist. Our conditional self or non-self questions, qualifies and gives names and forms occupying the relative positions. This conditional self is created, therefore it will not last forever. But when we come to the realization of the true Self we gain eternal, immortal life. To exist in God really means, in this relative plane to exist in the consciousness of God.

In what sense are we part of God? When we consider this conditional or created universe as a part of God. It has been proved that this universe neither can be God or a part of Him. Since we are a part of this universe by living in it, we cannot be a part of God also. Either we must be God in the Absolute sense or nothing. But if we take conditions which apparently limit the Absolute into parts, like the lines which describe forms in the space, we may consider ourselves part of God. But these parts are not real, but seeming.

(Comment: As the space which is walled in is considered to be a part of the eternal space, so we may consider ourselves as parts of the eternal principle, being limited by the conditions. As in the case of space, we know it never can be walled in, in the true sense of the word; since the uniform space can be found even in the walls so our real Self never can be limited by the conditions.)

Though in the relative or seeming sense we may consider ourselves parts of God, or God limited by the conditions, we always ought to bear in mind that in reality those parts are whole, since there cannot be any break in the Absolute. That which exists is the Absolute.

Relatively speaking that which exists, exists in dimension or space, therefore we can conceive its parts. But in the Absolute sense whatever is, always is and it does not change in form, shape, color, condition, space and time. It is beyond all attributes. Hence if it has any parts they always were and always will be even in the relative sense. But since these parts, if they exist at all, cannot be changeable, we being changeable cannot be these parts.

The non-self is like the shadow of the real Self. Its existence, however unreal and imaginary it may be, is dependent upon the real Self. Hence we say that its existence is derived from the source of the real Self. As we are liable to mistake a reflection for the real thing, so we are liable to mistake the non-self for the real Self. These words, shadow and reflection, have been used as figures of speech showing that the very unreal thing stands for, or represents some thing real.

(Comment: We cannot say a thing is unreal if it does not exist, though it may not exist in the permanent sense. The thing which does not exist does not require our denial or affirmation. According to this statement the unreal thing exists as a name or reflection of something real. In this sense, whatever we think or imagine, exists either as a reflection or as something real.)

As the non-self is not the real Self so the creation of non-self is not the real creation. But since we think that our non-self is the real Self its creation also is seemingly real to us.

What we are to-day is the result of the creation of our non-self. So we are creators of our own destiny or of ourselves. The creative power of the non-self is able to lead us to the realization of our real Self. Since non-self creates by imagination or by holding a clear picture of a thing or a condition, it can also create an ideal of perfection which may bring us the realization of our perfect real Self.

Non-self creates itself by creating a thing or a condition for it. While it is creating a thing or a condition by the thought or imagination it is transforming itself into the quality of the image it is holding in its mind.

(Comment: Another name for a quality is the value we put upon a thing, person or condition. This value transforms our non-self into its nature. By the continuous thought of a person we grow like him in quality. If that quality is true to his physical form, or it corresponds to it, we are liable to look like him both in quality and form. If an attributed quality does not correspond to a person, by thought of that quality we may embody the quality alone. Sometimes we may embody the form of the person too if we strongly associate that imaginary quality with his form. Many loving married couples by long association have grown to look like brother and sister. For the same reason we grow like our mental ideal both in quality and form, provided we hold that ideal firmly in our mind. It is not only true of our ideal alone, it is true of everything.)

Good and bad, both are the creation of non-self. Good and bad are determined by the values we put upon a thing or a condition. We put a value upon a thing or a condition according to our understanding or realization. Our understanding is relative, hence our understanding of good and bad is also relative; that is, it is subject to change.

———

By the relative value we determine good or bad. Good is that which is relatively superior to bad. Superior value means superior understanding. Without working against our own better understanding we cannot live a bad life by thinking it is good.

———

We can change our idea of good into bad and bad into good by changing their relative values. But that does not change the reaction of our relative understanding.

———

Our concept is our life. We can change our life by changing our concept.

———

The change does not always mean improvement. But the change which improves the relative value of a thing or a condition does certainly mean improvement.

———

The superior idea or value of a thing or a condition gives our non-self superior creative power. Hence love is the greater creative power than hate. It means unity, and it widens our lives by adding all unto us.

———

Every man is a law unto himself. The name of this law is cause and effect. As we sow so shall we reap. Every act reacts on us according to our concept of the act.

———

As a reaction is just in proportion to an action so an action is in exact proportion to our understanding. Our action never supersedes our understanding.

———

Our conscience is our better understanding. Our action is measured by our conscience. When we ignore our conscience we sin against our nature.

In the absolute sense there is no such thing called law. The law which we discovered in this relative plane is nothing but a relative standard by which we measure the unfoldment of our being. We recognize the law by our concept. In fact our concept determines the existence of this law.

(Comment: We know that there is no fixed law that governs the human life. The fact that no two persons equally suffer by violating the same law conclusively proves that there is no fixed law governing the human being. All our actions are justified by our concept, but not by a fixed law. If this concept means the law then this law is changeable, since our concept is changeable.)

The relative concept is sometimes called the law of evolution. As a part does not mean the whole, so a part of the non-self does not mean the whole of it. Consequently a part of the evolutionary law is applied to a part of the non-self. This part of the non-self is the part we consider ourselves to be. This part concept determines how the law shall act upon us. Therefore this law acts upon us according to our understanding of the problem of our life.

It has been already remarked that good is the improvement upon bad, and this improvement is determined by the relative value we put upon the terms, good and bad. In this sense nothing can be called absolutely bad. When we make an improvement upon yesterday's good, its relative value depreciates and we may call it bad. But in reality there is no such condition called bad. It is always good and better.

When good appears bad to us our action ought to be regulated by our superior understanding, if we want to avoid reaction, called suffering.

In the opinion of some people God is Law, and when we break this law we bring suffering upon us. If the law is God

130

then He is that power and potency which regulates our relative existence. He is then our concept of good, or better understanding. With the increase of the relative value of our life and understanding we come to the realization of our true Self.

If the imagination is the motive power in man, can he by the help of imagination control the effect of a reaction? Not directly by imagination. Reaction always follows an action without fail. We can alter the effect of it by our superior understanding. A thing or a condition affects us just in proportion to the value we attach to it. By changing the value of a reaction by our superior understanding we can avoid its effect. We only fail in changing the value of reaction, when we are conscious of the value of its action.

We disqualify or forfeit our better understanding by the repeated inferior thought or action. By the quality of thought we become like the thought we think, or we change into that which we imagine strongly. On account of the retrogression which follows our inferior thoughts or imaginations we are unable to change the effect of a reaction. The superior or inferior thought is determined by one's understanding.

It is not only true that as we think so we become, but it is also true, what we think, that we are.

(Comment: Our thought determines our relative existence. We think, therefore we exist. The nature of a thought is the indication of the nature of our being, consequently what we think, that we are.)

By living the higher life we rise above the reaction of an inferior action.

The imagination has two distinct qualities; transformation

and reproduction. It can transform us into its quality and also reproduce the quality which becomes a part of us.

The power of imagination is determined by the degree of realization we have about it. The whole mystery of the creation lies buried in the word understanding.

Any imagination beyond our comprehension is non-productive. We can never materialize an imagination without understanding its relative value.

Our purely mental grasp or comprehension is not the realization, it simply indicates the possibility of our future success.

Nothing comes to us if we do not create the condition for it. When the right condition is created within us our desires are fulfilled.

If we create a condition for something consciously or unconsciously it is bound to come, whether we want it or not. The affinity for a thing really means the affinity for its condition.

The word vibration means in the metaphysical sense the consciousness of our being. We raise our vibration by raising our consciousness. When we reach a desired object by our vibration we form an affinity with it.

We raise or lower our vibration by raising or lowering our consciousness. By the imagination or thought we raise or lower our consciousness.

We relate our consciousness with an object by imagining that it belongs to us. That is the only conscious method to create a condition for an object or condition.

When we desire any thing we desire the condition or value of it. Therefore, sometimes the exact thing we desire may not come to us, but the thing of that nature or condition may come. The faster we vibrate with a desired object or relate it with our consciousness the sooner it will come to us.

There is but one mind, and we call this mind conscious and sub-conscious mind. That part of the consciousness, of which we have not come to the conscious realization, we mistakenly call sub-conscious mind. This sub-conscious mind is just as much conscious, or infinitely more so, than our conscious mind. We may rather call it Cosmic Consciousness than sub-conscious mind. The faculty of mind is thinking, but the Cosmic Consciousness which is a perfect and self-knowing power has no need of thinking. Our self-knowing consciousness or conscious mind is the manifestation of the great Cosmic Consciousness through our concept.

To the extent we realize Cosmic Consciousness we are conscious of our own self. All of us have not the same degree of consciousness. The only way we can come to the fullest realization of Cosmic Consciousness is to know our real Self.

The instinct is the sum total of our stored up past experiences. We may forget these experiences in detail but we carry their impressions in our action and thought.

We generally conceive the idea of a part out of a whole, but seldom the idea of a whole out of its part. Hence our right concept about the conscious mind is that it is a part of the Cosmic Consciousness. The power which seems to be latent within us is really self-manifested. Nothing can be added to or be taken from it. The consciousness of which you are unconscious, not which is unconscious, can be called subconscious mind in the relative sense. This mind, though consciousness itself takes no part in our conscious action. The consciousness which has to come to the realization of more consciousness needs to act towards perfection. We become conscious of the Cosmic Consciousness to a degree we believe it is manifesting through us.

We wake up that so-called latent subconscious force within us, by the imagination that it is waking up. In this world of concept an idea or a thought always manifests its quality through us if we invite it to our mental realm, and do not disturb its serenity.

When we are absorbed in a subject and dwell upon it without any mental strain we call it subjective concentration. When special effort is necessary to keep our mind on a subject we call it objective concentration. When objective concentration becomes subjective it becomes effective.

Whenever by holding one idea in our mind we become oblivious to the conscious activity of our mind we unconsciously reach the great subconscious realm. The principal point in meditation is to concentrate subjectively upon an Ideal by the reduction of the conscious activity of the conscious mind.

In a degree we are successful in concentrating upon the effect of a cause we gain the desired result. The effect which is principally sought must be held fast in our minds as if it were reality or materialized.

From The Relative to The Absolute

Spirit and matter are one. The same thing is called by two different names. When we see matter we see spirit. Only one thing exists, no matter by what name we call it. Since we call it spirit there cannot exist any thing else called matter. Hence matter is another name for spirit. If matter is not the right name for spirit it is the wrong name. A wrong name cannot change the real thing. It means the real thing just as much as the right name. Therefore spirit and matter are one.

A name without the object it stands for is meaningless and it cannot exist. Hence matter does not exist by itself without the absolute intelligence whose name it is supposed to be.

If the word matter means limitation or condition it cannot mean the Absolute. Because the Absolute is beyond all limitation, time, space, and condition.

Since a name has no meaning without the thing it stands for, it must stand for a definite thing it designates. If the word matter means something limited, it cannot be spirit, absolute, which means limitless. Since nothing can exist but the Absolute Spirit the thing which we call matter cannot exist.

(*Comment: The thing, matter, as a limited object cannot exist, since the absolute spirit is All in All. Now if we recognize matter in the same sense as we recognize a wall in a space, then it exists only in our concept. The real significance of the wall depends upon our recognition of the fact that space can be walled in, so the existence of matter depends upon our recognition, that the Absolute Spirit can be limited. Had we not had the recognition*

135

of the wall from our relative concept we would not have admitted its existence. We know that space cannot be walled in in reality, since it exists even in the very walls. Hence a wall has no other significance than what we believe it to be. So matter has no significance.)

By the concentrated imagination we can create such walls around us as will give us the same sense of resistance as so called objective walls. By hypnotic suggestion which is nothing but the stimulation of imagination we can put an imaginary barrier before a man which will seem to him as real as an objective barrier. In order to deny that imaginary barrier that man will have to come out of that influence, so also will we have to come out of the influence of matter in order to find, that there is no matter in the sense we believe it. Imagination, according to our understanding, is the first step to free ourselves from the bondage of matter.

It is the imagination which makes our task easy and difficult. We can reach God and feel His Presence if we can imagine that it is natural and easy.

Anything in action moves. Mind in action, which we call thinking also moves. We can move our mind in any direction by the concentrated imagination. When our mind moves in any direction it moves with its thought picture. This is what is our experience in this relative plane.

Every impulse which our mind receives by thinking goes to create a condition, according to the nature or quality of the thought. Therefore thought or imagination always creates a vortex of a condition which brings about change in our whole being. By the concentrated imagination we attune our mind with another mind in the relative sense. Whenever our imagination makes us feel a condition we become that condition. We must first be acquainted with a condition of another mind before we try to create that condition within us by the concentrated imagination. When any two minds are of the same or similar condition they are attuned with each other.

As our action is judged by our motive, so our motive is judged by the imaginary value we put upon it. If the motive of our action is far above our comprehension it cannot regulate the effect of an action.

We partake of the nature of the thought and thing we think of. Even when we deny an object, with the recognition of its certain value we partake of its nature.

All conditions are unreal in the permanent sense. Since they exist in our ideas it is by changing one idea for another we obtain things and conditions we desire.

We live in the world of ideas, in other words the world of conditions. Therefore we live in a temporal or unreal world. The good and bad are relative conditions, therefore they are changeable and unreal.

Different people have different ideas regarding things and conditions. Therefore they affect them according to their ideas.

Since one idea takes the place of another it is natural for us to change our idea to suit the demand of our being. The real significance of this life is the continuous action, to change our lower ideas for higher ideas, according to our understanding.

All other ideas except the abstract idea of the eternal spirit are unreal. If that be the case, is it not a fact that our very abstract idea of spirit is limited by our personal idea? Consequently our idea of real cannot be real after all, since it is an idea of imperfect man. But if the idea of the real is the highest and best ideal we can conceive of, then its moral effect is certainly very great and elevating. Because we partake of the nature of the thought we think.

———

By acting the part of our ideal we become it. Because acting stimulates our mind and helps to form a vortex of a condition.

(*Comment: We cannot act the part of our ideal if we are conscious of our own shortcomings and weaknesses. Nothing keeps us from materializing our desires as self-consciousness. The way to overcome self-consciousness is to think less of it and think more of the higher power which is trying to manifest through us.*)

———

It is waste of time to think what we are not. The more conscious we are of what we are not, the less we succeed in being what we want to be.

———

This world is real to us because we accept the evidences of our senses by our thought. If we lose all our consciousness about it it will cease to exist to us. The existence of a thing depends upon our recognition of it.

———

Since good is not bad according to our understanding, real cannot be unreal for the same reason. Though the real and unreal both may be unreal from the absolute standpoint of view, they cannot be the same to our relative concept, because their relative values are not the same.

———

The real is a condition, so is unreal. They are nothing but the change of condition.

———

What we strive for in this life is the condition which we think now to be the highest and the best.

The thing without the value we put on it, does not affect us. In fact, things are not what they seem, but what we think them to be.

The best and highest idea we can have in this relative plane, is that God is All in All. His power is manifesting through us. There cannot exist anything but God in this world of God. He is perfect, and everything is His manifestation. "I and my Father are one."

There is no such condition called disease in this world of All-health, God, except what our thinking makes. By recognizing a condition we make it reality to us. This, our creative power can create for us any condition we desire.

If disease and health suggest each other we ought to forget them both by giving the full right of way to our great Ideal, God, to guide our life.

It is through the higher idea we gain the higher consciousness. The name of that idea is God, the Soul of our Souls. This idea, God, is always the same. He is the sum total of energy of this universe. We always belong to Him and our consciousness is His consciousness.

According to the higher concept of life in this relative plane we consider our action God's action, not as whole but as part. The whole acts as a whole and a part as part. There is a great difference between the two actions. The whole acts in all its parts, but parts act within their own limits.

If God is unchangeable why do we change as His part? No, we do not change in reality. We are always the same as the essence of God. But we expand ourselves in consciousness from the smaller part to the greater part.

What do we mean when we say we are parts of God? We are parts of God by our part consciousness of our real self. Only that which is conscious of its own existence exists in reality. Since we are conscious of our own existence in part we are parts of that which is Self-existent, eternal, immortal principle.

———

Does God think, or has He the impression of thought when He acts? No; His action is not dependent on thought. Thought is the action of the mind or the part consciousness. As long as the part consciousness will not arrive at its full consciousness so long it will act. Its very attempt to reach the perfect consciousness indicates its action. But the All-perfect God acts by living or being, but not by doing.

———

If the action of the parts is the action of God, why do His parts think and He does not? Our consciousness of being is our action, so it is with God, our consciousness of being is the part consciousness of the whole. That part consciousness wants the full realization. The very desire for the expansion of the consciousness or knowledge gives birth to thought. A part, as long as it is a part cannot realize the entire nature of the whole. But it can realize its own nature, which is similar, though not the same as that of the whole. A part is not the whole, though the whole is in part and more. A part exists in the whole, and the whole exists in a part. So we being parts of God, live, move and have our being in Him, in our consciousness.

———

Existence which is beyond time, space and condition is God, the highest ideal concept of man. Man is nothing but his consciousness or concept. In this sense man is God limited and God is man unlimited, since God is the only perfect consciousness.

———

There is no other law than that which a man recognizes for himself. A man recognizes a law according to his concept of life. So every man is a law unto himself. The law which we recognize we must live up to, if we want to be happy.

The word love means unity, therefore we consider it to be the highest law in this universe.

It is the way of sense-man to follow the path of sex and senses, but the way of God-man is to live up to his highest concept of life in thought and action.

When we are not true to ourselves we break the law of our being. This law of being is the law of our consciousness or concept. It is always the same.

They say this law of our being is the law of cause and effect. Where there is an action there is a reaction. This reaction is of the same nature as the action. We ought to always remember that our action has no other significance than that which we attribute to it. We interpret the significance of an action according to our concept of things and actions. Our concept changes according to our growth and expansion. In other words, our concept is just in proportion to our growth.

There is no within or without to man. He represents a certain stage of consciousness. By thoughts and actions he creates conditions which manifest the whole man as we see him. His physical body and mind are one. They are both the manifestation of his consciousness. By changing his consciousness or concept we can change the whole man. In order to change one's body and mind we treat his consciousness.

Disease is defective consciousness or concept, judging by one's better understanding. By turning the light of divine power upon one's concept we can make up his defect. A person who treats a person's body thinking it a seat of disease can never cure a disease in the real sense of the term. He is as far removed from the truth as pole from pole. It is not the question of denying or admitting the existence of the physical body, but it is the question of the defective concept of being.

When we treat any disease at a distance we do not send the patient the healing thought, but we raise ourselves in our higher consciousness and desire the cure or change of his concept. In order to treat a person we must receive him in our consciousness with the idea that his consciousness is changing like ours. Our consciousness or concept is what we believe to be the real life. By the association with our larger concept of life a sick person, if anxious to receive light, is born again both in spirit and body. Let any sick person give himself up to the care of our Ideal or higher concept of life, and he will be whole. The same result can be obtained if we ask the help of our Ideal with proper faith and understanding.

The words positive and negative are generally used as polar opposites. The negative is not negation of positive, but it is less positive. So are the light and darkness, disease and health, and all other supposed polar opposites.

They say the light is the positive manifestation. So it is true of our being, when we have the light or understanding, it manifests positive quality.

Every thing is divine and spiritual if we can make it. "There is nothing either good or bad, but thinking makes it so." As light illumines the dark spot, so our divine concept spiritualizes a thing and action.

We live in the feeling. We get that feeling by imagination. We demonstrate power according to our capacity of

142

feeling it. Our capacity is determined by our concept or consciousness.

The idea of perfection as an idea is one of the grandest ideas human mind can conceive of. It is not the question of perfection in reality, but it is the question of idea which sustains our relative existence. Since all our ideas are relative, our idea of perfection cannot be any thing but relative; that means limited or imperfect. But the idea changes the idea, and perfection is reached by the higher idea of perfection. Then the idea that we are living, moving and having our being in the perfect God is the grandest idea we can ever hold in our mind.

All that is drawn to us is due to the conditions which we consciously or unconsciously create within us. It explains why sometimes a thing happens to us, when we do not look for it. If the poison takes effect on us when we take it unknowingly, it is because there is a condition in our concept which invites that effect. By changing our concept we can one day rise above the effect of the poison.

The real and unreal are conditions, both of which exist in our concept. Only one relatively exists for the other, unreal for the real. What is unreal now stands for some thing real. Similarly what is real now may be unreal by our recognition of a still better condition. Without assuming the existence of some thing real we cannot say a certain thing is unreal. Because we judge a thing or a condition by comparison. Above these real and unreal conditions stands the Absolute, God, the great Cosmic Consciousness. Our consciousness of our self is a part consciousness of that which alone exists beyond time, space, condition and form. He is our Life and Christian Yoga is the way.

To The Followers of Truth

Always listen with patience and sympathy to those whose understanding is inferior to yours. Never make them feel that they do not know anything.

A man who is sincere and willing to learn is better than the one who thinks that he knows all. Even a rich man may enter into the kingdom of God, but a proud egotist never will. According to the Master Jesus we must be like little children in order to see the kingdom of God.

Take all unjust criticisms silently. Never try to vindicate yourself by words. Let your actions speak louder than your words. You cannot convince a man if he is set in his opinion.

Do not argue with anyone about the truth. Truth is self-evident. None can know it by reason. Only by living the right life and realization do we know the truth.

When anyone asks any question in order to learn, answer it as best you can. If you are not satisfied with your own answer, then refer him to someone whom you think can give the best answer. Always be humble regarding truth.

The spirit of learning is no sign of ignorance. A man acquires half the knowledge when he is willing to learn.

Do not be over-anxious for your success, because success comes to those who deserve it. Therefore trust in the Almighty for the result and live a deserving life.

Never underrate the value of the silent work. Our public work always bears testimony to our silent work. Always gather force and power in silence without any spirit of competition and always look within for help and inspiration. The thing which we have not we cannot give. We must have the realization of the truth first before we venture to give it. "Thou shalt not steal" some other person's thoughts and use them only for the glory. Try to understand and realize them and they will be your own by your Divine rights.

All knowledge and wisdom are within man. By silent meditation he can acquire them. Do not meditate upon what somebody else has said and written, but meditate upon the subject your soul is hungry for or wants to know.

If you want to know what is best for you to do, do not think and fret over it, just be calm and quiet and wait for the inner direction; it will come without fail. While waiting for the direction never anticipate any definite answer.

Know this that the way of God is different from man. When we trust in Him he leads us safely through the dangers and difficulties in an unforeseen way. The dangers and difficulties come and go, but our soul is never anchored more securely than when we trust in the Almighty power within us.

When all the external means fail, the invisible power never fails. Remember that many people have been saved from shipwreck in mid-ocean. Never fear as long as you can think of God's presence within you. Trust and fear cannot abide in the same place.

Do not regret your false steps. Thank God that you are alive and can take the right steps. Some people are so dead that they cannot take any steps whatever. Are you not more fortunate than they?

Never neglect anyone no matter how inferior he may be. Who knows he is not a great man in his place. He may be still greater some day. God Almighty's children have the equal right to enjoy the fruit of their labor. Do not deprive them of their own earnings by your unbrotherly acts.

Show no spite to those who slander you; instead, bless them, because they know not what they are doing. You cannot spite your fellow brothers and sisters without spiting yourself, because we all live, move and have our being in one God.

If a man sincerely believes he has the truth, do not doubt it, because the fountainhead of truth is within man. It is his privilege to claim his own divine heritage.

If you have not found peace within your soul you have not found the truth. If jealousy still gnaws your heart, public opinion sways your mind hither and thither, and if you seek glory first, before you have done your work, then know that you are far from the truth.

Remember this, that truth is one and eternal. If any one by following the truth does some good works, send him your helpful thought. Envy him not because he is possessed of truth. Do you not know that he has labored in the Lord's vineyard while you were sleeping away your time? It is his rightful earning, let him enjoy it.

The man who is poor in heart is poor indeed in spite of all his wealth. He lives in the world of fear to lose what he has. He can never demonstrate the spiritual law which requires copiousness of heart. We cannot be half way material and half way spiritual, if we want to reach the great reservoir of spiritual knowledge. When we are through and through spiritual even the very material things become spiritual by

146

our touch. Then and then alone we come to realize that spirit and matter are one, and we live, move and have our being in God. That is the only eternal bliss and the only supreme realization.

What difference does it make whether the people call us material or spiritual? If you have not the peace in your mind, know it for certain, that you are not living the life you ought to live, according to your better understanding. Somehow or other you are limiting your nature. It may be your love of approbation, of wealth, or name and fame. Whatever it may be, until you break through the shell you will never be in peace. Resist not your divine nature to thrive. Let it grow in the free atmosphere of the living God. Remember that you and your God are one.

Never give any thought to what you shall eat and wear. They give no spiritual unfoldment. Those who are attached to the external ceremonies and forms cannot rise above them, because we partake of the nature of a thought, thing, or person we think of. Spiritual unfoldment must be sought free from all external means.

The mind which seeks external ceremonies will find them, and the mind which seeks God will find Him.

Hold the thought of success for others and you will have success, because your every thought reflects back on you.

Send your best thought to all, and you will receive the best in return.

Friends and followers of Christian Yoga! Remember this: Whatever we deserve comes to us. Every thing moves in this universe by an invisible law. Think not of the external conditions and means, but look within and live the deserving life. Whatever you desire will come to you in the right time in response to the conditions you have created within yourself. If you want to understand the great spiritual law, have first calmness, peace and poise. Know this, that you cannot move even a feather if you do not deserve the power to do it. Why then should you worry about anything in this world? Just simply live the deserving life, every thing you desire will come to you. Do not envy your friend's position; he is getting what he deserves. If that position is forced upon you and you do not deserve it, you will not be able to command it. Therefore, we say, live the deserving life; even the angels will come down from heaven to assist you.

Have you any shortcoming? Then do not think of it. Think as much as possible that your perfect Ideal is manifesting through you and you are changing into your Ideal. As we think so we become.

The best way to get rid of a disease is neither to deny nor to admit it. Both the denial and admittance compel our attention to the very thing we want to be rid of. Only let your Ideal, perfect Health, take possession of you and manifest through you.

Have you ever heard the voice from within? If not, then retire within yourself and you will hear it. Ask that voice any question you want to, it will answer you. If you want the right direction for your life or anything, simply ask; do not anticipate any definite answer, the right answer will come. "Whatsoever ye shall ask in prayer, believing, ye shall receive."

Let your disposition and manner always show that you are following the banner of truth. Never fail to show childlike simplicity to admit when you think you are wrong.

148

When you pray, pray for the simple trust in the all-providing Law. When you have the trust you have every thing at your disposal.

Do not listen to what the people say about you, good or bad, if you want to maintain peace in your mind. Just silently do the work of your Ideal and trust in its all-providing power. Always give the credit for your work to your Ideal.

Trusting in God try to get a glimpse of the spiritual knowledge. The man who once has the glimpse of spiritual knowledge cannot go back to materialism. Something in man's nature revolts against any action contrary to his better understanding. He can never be happy again if he turns his back against the truth he understands.

Instead of brooding over adversity, if you try to imagine the good fortune which is awaiting you, you will accomplish more towards the betterment of your condition than otherwise. Misfortune does not exist beyond your recognition. By imagining the better condition awaiting you, you give recognition to that condition, which counteracts the recognition of adverse conditions. Imagination does not so much suggest the condition of polar opposites as a fixed affirmation.

Speak always kind to those who antagonize you, because thereby you will win their love and sympathy.

Some people will come to you to test your power of healing. Always receive them kindly and tell them that the power belongs to the Almighty God. Those who are willing to be healed, trusting in His Power will be healed and none else.

Listen not to the person who speaks ill of your friend or so-called foe. Remember, it always creates a mental disturbance and lowers the spiritual concept of both the speaker and listener.

Do not compare your achievement with that of your neighbor. Every one of us ought to be satisfied with our work if we have done our best. The spirit of comparison always inspires competition. In the harvest field of spiritual knowledge none ought to recognize any competition. Where brotherly love is the motto, competition ought not to exist.

All names, ceremonies and forms will pass away, but the truth we preach will survive forever.

Welcome everybody among you in the name of the Master. Give the credit for all your worthy actions to your Ideal. Radiate the spirit of love and good will wherever you go. Ask the Divine Intelligence to guide you always. Peace be with you!

Triumph of the Human Spirit:
The Greatest Achievements of the Human Soul and How Its Power can Change Your Life
by Paul Tice.

This book is about those who changed the entire course of history. They did not start with money, power, or great armies—all they had was an idea, and a passion for the truth. Gandhi, Joan of Arc, Dr. King and others died for their ideas but made the world a better place. This book outlines how an intuitive spiritual knowledge, or "gnosis," provided these people with guidance and helped to create the most incredible spiritual moments that the world has ever known. These events are all part of our spiritual evolution. We have learned from past mistakes, have become more tolerant toward others, and the people in this book have been signposts——pointing us collectively toward something greater. This book also shows how a spiritual triumph of your own can be achieved. Various exercises will strengthen the soul and reveal its hidden power. Unlike the past, in today's Western world we are free to explore the truth without fear of being tortured or executed. As a result, the rewards are great. This is the perfect book for all those who believe in spiritual freedom and have a passion for the truth.

BT-574 · ISBN 1-885395-57-4 · 295 pages
6 x 9 · trade paper · illustrated · $19.95

Buddhist Suttas: Major Scriptural Writings from Early Buddhism
by T.W. Rhys Davids.

These seven scriptural writings are considered by many to be the most important of the Buddhist religion. Originally written in the Pali language, they date to the fourth and third centuries BC. This early date is what makes them so important—they form the very core of Buddhist teachings. The influence of the texts contained in this book upon the entire Buddhist world is enormous. They have been sought after and studied by monks and scholars for centuries, and there could never be a complete understanding of the true meaning of Buddhism without them. This collection of texts was not only translated by the great T.W. Rhys Davids, but edited by the renowned scholar of eastern religions, F. Max Muller, making it clearly the most reliable text of its kind in the English language.

BT-794 · ISBN 1-58509-079-4 · 376 pages
6 x 9 · trade paper · $27.95

Lightning Source UK Ltd.
Milton Keynes UK
UKHW011849130223
416874UK00001B/94

9 781585 090402